Best Easy Day Hikes Series

Best Easy Day Hikes
Spokane /
Coeur d'Alene

Fred Barstad

FALCONGUIDES

GUILFORD, CONNECTICUT
HELENA, MONTANA

AN IMPRINT OF GLOBE PEQUOT PRESS

FALCONGUIDES®

Copyright © 2012 Morris Book Publishing, LLC

ALL RIGHTS RESERVED. No part of this book may be reproduced or transmitted in any form by any means, electronic or mechanical, including photocopying and recording, or by any information storage and retrieval system, except as may be expressly permitted in writing from the publisher. Requests for permission should be addressed to Globe Pequot Press, Attn: Rights and Permissions Department, PO Box 480, Guilford, CT 06437.

FalconGuides is an imprint of Globe Pequot Press.
Falcon, FalconGuides, and Outfit Your Mind are registered trademarks of Morris Book Publishing, LLC.

Project editor: Julie Marsh
Layout: Joanna Beyer
Maps: Daniel Lloyd © Morris Book Publishing, LLC
TOPO! Explorer software and SuperQuad source maps courtesy of National Geographic Maps. For information about TOPO! Explorer, TOPO!, and Nat Geo Maps products, go to www.topo.com or www.natgeomaps.com.

Library of Congress Cataloging-in-Publication Data

Barstad, Fred.
  Best easy day hikes Spokane/Coeur d'Alene / Fred Barstad.
      p. cm.
  ISBN 978-0-7627-7363-3
  1. Hiking—Washington (State)—Spokane Region—Guidebooks. 2. Hiking—Idaho—Coeur d'Alene Region—Guidebooks. 3. Spokane Region (Wash.)—Guidebooks. 4. Coeur d'Alene Region (Idaho)—Guidebooks. I. Title.
  GV199.42.W22S642 2012
  796.510979—dc23

2012008251

Printed in the United States of America

Contents

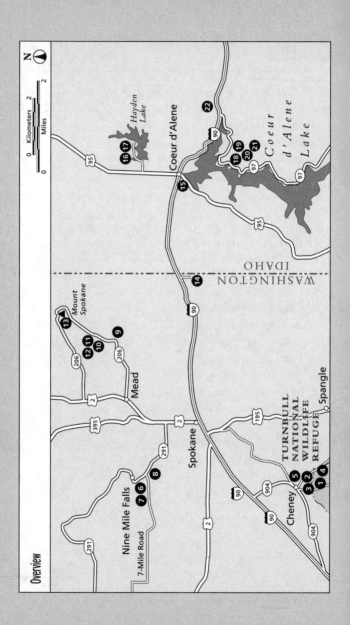

Overview

N

0 Kilometers 2
0 Miles 2

Hayden Lake

Coeur d'Alene

16 17

95

22

90

18 19
20 21
97

Coeur d'Alene Lake

97

95

15?

95

WASHINGTON
IDAHO

14

90

Mount Spokane

13

206

12 11
10

9

206

2

395

Mead

291

2

Nine Mile Falls

8

7 6

7-Mile Road

291

Spokane

2

90

90

904

TURNBULL NATIONAL WILDLIFE REFUGE

5

2

3

1 4

Cheney

904

195

Spangle

90

Acknowledgments

Thanks to the people from the land management agencies who reviewed portions of my text: Lori Cobb from Riverside State Park, Steve Cristenson from Mount Spokane State Park, Sandy Rancourt from Turnbull National Wildlife Refuge, and Brian White from the Bureau of Land Management.

Thanks to Alex Hoppe for joining me while collecting information.

Most of all thanks to my wife, Sue Barstad, for all her computer help.

Help Us Keep This Guide Up to Date

Every effort has been made by the author and editors to make this guide as accurate and useful as possible. However, many things can change after a guide is published—trails are rerouted, regulations change, facilities come under new management, etc.

We would appreciate hearing from you concerning your experiences with this guide and how you feel it could be improved and kept up to date. While we may not be able to respond to all comments and suggestions, we'll take them to heart and we'll also make certain to share them with the author. Please send your comments and suggestions to the following address:

GPP
Reader Response/Editorial Department
P.O. Box 480
Guilford, CT 06437

Or you may e-mail us at:

editorial@GlobePequot.com

Thanks for your input, and happy trails!

Introduction

The Spokane House, close to the Little Spokane River, was the earliest non–Native American settlement in the Pacific Northwest. Established in 1810, the little trading post was widely known for its hospitality and is now in Riverside State Park. In 1872 the city of Spokane, currently Washington's second largest, was established about 10 miles south of the Spokane House next to Spokane Falls on the Spokane River.

In 1878 Civil War general William Tecumseh Sherman established an army post at what is now Coeur d'Alene, next to the spot where the Spokane River leaves Coeur d'Alene Lake. From that beginning the city of Coeur d'Alene grew to what it is today, getting a boost in the 1880s by the boom in the Silver Valley Mining District to the east.

If you live in the Spokane / Coeur d'Alene area, you have a wide array of hiking opportunities at your doorstep. From the semiarid Columbia Plateau, to the timbered slopes of Mount Coeur d'Alene and Mineral Ridge, and higher to the subalpine summit of Mount Spokane, hiking is available nearly year-round. If you are a visitor to the area, take the time to explore the possibilities. This book really just gives the hiker a taste of what is available close to these beautiful cities.

The Nature of the Spokane / Coeur d'Alene Area

Spokane is at 1,900 feet elevation, near the poorly defined boundary between the grass and sagebrush of the semiarid Palouse Prairie to the southwest and the timbered plateau and well-watered mountains to the north and east. In general, rainfall (and snowfall) increases as you go farther east (toward Coeur d'Alene) and/or gain altitude in this part of the Northwest. In Spokane the average January high temperature is 33°F and the average low is 22°F. The average July high temperature is 82°F and the average low is 55°F. The city of Coeur d'Alene sits at 2,160 feet elevation in the pines next to beautiful Coeur d'Alene Lake. Coeur d'Alene is generally slightly cooler and wetter than Spokane.

Critters
Deer and elk are common along most of the hikes included in this guide. These are generally docile animals, but both the bucks and the bulls can be somewhat aggressive during the fall rut (breeding season). Some cow elk seem to have a strong dislike for dogs and occasionally cause injuries. Bears and cougars are not often seen but are possible on all the hikes described here. Moose sightings are also possible on many of the hikes. Moose are large animals that should never be closely approached or challenged in any way. Rattlesnakes are possible on all but the highest elevation hikes in this book, and ticks can be a problem in the spring and summer.

Be Prepared
Even on the easy hikes, weather conditions can change rapidly. The danger of adverse weather generally increases with elevation and the length of the hike. Always take clothes that are adequate for all possible conditions. Water, food, and a map should be taken along on all but the shortest hikes. A guidebook and GPS receiver are also very handy. Cell phone service can generally be had on at least part of most of the hikes described here.

Following are a few simple things you can do that will improve your chances of staying healthy while you are on your hikes:

First, check the weather report before heading into the mountains. Afternoon and evening thunderstorms are common from spring through early fall and can include heavy rain and hail as well as lightning. If a storm is approaching, get off ridgelines if possible and retreat to your car. Protective clothing is always a good idea.

Know the symptoms of both cold- and heat-related conditions, including hypothermia, heat stroke, and heat exhaustion. The easiest way to avoid these afflictions is to wear proper clothing, dress in layers, and keep adequately fed and hydrated.

On all but the shortest hikes, carry a backpack for your extra clothing and gear. This is much more comfortable than trying to carry this stuff in your hands.

Inform friends or relatives of your plans and when you plan to return.

If you are planning a long or difficult hike, be sure to get into shape ahead of time. This will make your trip much more pleasant as well as safer.

Know the basics of first aid, including how to treat bleeding, bites and stings, and strains or sprains. Always pack a first-aid kit.

One of the most important things to do is to be careful about your drinking water supply. On most of these hikes the best thing to do is to take along all the water you will need from a known safe source. All surface water should be filtered, chemically treated, or boiled before drinking.

If you have children along, keep a close eye on them. A few of the hikes described here have cliffs or steep drop-offs close to the trail. In some places stinging and/or poisonous plants are present, and there is always the chance, even though slim, of meeting a rattler. Children should carry a whistle to use if they are lost—and only if they are lost.

Of all the safety tips, the most important is to take your brain with you when you venture into the wilds. Without it no tips will help, and with it almost any obstacle can be avoided or overcome. Think about what you're doing, be safe, and have a great time in the outdoors.

Meeting Stock or Mountain Bikers

Meeting stock traffic is not a common occurrence on most of the trails described here. It is possible, however, on a few of them, so it's a good idea to know how to pass stock with the least possible disturbance or danger. If you meet parties with stock, try to get as far off the trail as possible. Horsemen prefer that you stand on the downhill side of the trail, but there is some question as to whether this is the safest place for a hiker. If possible, I like to get well off the trail on the uphill side. It is often a good idea to talk quietly to the horses and their riders, as this seems to calm many horses. If you have a dog with you, be sure to keep it restrained and quiet. Read the "Canine compatibility" section at the beginning of each hike description to get information about including your dog on that particular hike.

Mountain bikers use many of the trails covered in this book. It is the responsibility of bikers to yield to other users, but in some rare cases they may not see a hiker quickly enough to prevent a collision. Bikes are quiet, so the hiker should keep a careful watch for their approach. Read the "Other trail users" section at the beginning of each hike description to find out whether the trail you are going to hike is open to other users.

Leave No Trace

Many of the trails in the Spokane / Coeur d'Alene region are heavily used. As trail users, we must be vigilant to make sure our passing leaves no lasting mark. Here are some basic guidelines for preserving the trails in our region:

- Pack out all trash, including biodegradable items like orange peels. You might also pack out garbage left by other less considerate hikers.
- Don't pick wildflowers or pick up rocks or antlers along the trail. Leave these things for others to also enjoy.
- Don't cut switchbacks, which can promote erosion.
- Be courteous by not making loud noises while hiking.
- Many of these trails are multiuse, which means that you will share them with runners, bikers, and/or equestrians. Familiarize yourself with proper trail etiquette, and yield the trail when appropriate.
- If possible, use the restrooms at the trailhead; if not, dispose of waste properly, well away from the trail and any water.

For more information on Leave No Trace hiking, visit www.LNT.org.

Getting around the Spokane / Coeur d'Alene Area

All of the hikes in this guide are well under an hour's drive from either Spokane or Coeur d'Alene. The I-90 freeway traverses the region from west to east. All of the driving directions begin at an exit off I-90 or from downtown Spokane at the junction of I-90 and Division Street.

Maps

Up-to-date maps for the hikes that are included in this guide seem to be difficult to obtain. In most cases the maps provided in this book are adequate for hiking the trails described. Other maps are recommended at the beginning of each hike description. In many cases USGS quad maps and the National Geographic topo maps on CD-ROM don't show the trails described here and, with a few exceptions, are not recommended for these hikes. The *Riverside State Park Multi-use Trails Map,* produced by the Inland Empire Backcountry Horsemen, is an excellent map for hikes in Riverside State Park, and the map in the Turnbull National Wildlife Refuge brochure is a good one for the hikes on the refuge. Often there will be a map on a reader board at the trailhead, which will be helpful.

A Note about State Highway Designations

In Washington the state highways are designated SR for "state route." In Idaho the state highways are designated SH for "state highway." This book uses these designations in accordance with each state's maps and road signs.

Land Management

All the hikes in this book are located on public lands. These lands are managed by several different agencies. The Pine Lakes Loop, Stubblefield Lake Loop, 30 Acre Lake, and Blackhorse Lake Boardwalk hikes are on the Turnbull National Wildlife Refuge, managed by the United States Fish and Wildlife Service. Riverside State Park, part of Washington's fantastic state park system, includes the Deep Creek Bench Loop, Deep Creek Overlook Loop, and Bowl and Pitcher Loop. Mount Spokane State Park, another of

Washington's great state parks, includes the Entrance Loop, Mount Kit Carson, Burping Brook Loop, Bald Knob–CCC Cabin, and Mount Spokane Summit–Saddle Junction hikes. The United States Department of the Interior, Bureau of Land Management (BLM) manages the ground beneath the Mineral Ridge, Lost Man, Caribou Ridge, and Mount Coeur d'Alene hikes. The Liberty Creek Loop is in the Liberty Lake Regional Park, which is managed by Spokane County Parks and Recreation. The United States Department of Agriculture Forest Service oversees the trails at English Point and the Mullan Military Road. Washington State Parks and Recreation Commission manages the Columbia Plateau Trail.

How to Use This Guide

This guide is designed to be as easy to use as possible. Each hike description contains a map and summary information that includes the hike's distance, difficulty, surface, and required fees and permits. The distance represents the entire recommended hike, including any side trips and both legs of an out-and-back route. Options add additional mileage. Also addressed are canine compatibility, approximate hiking time, best seasons, other trail users, hours that the route is open, and trail contacts. Directions to the trailhead and what to expect along the trail are also covered. The Miles and Directions section at the end of each hike description provides mileages between significant points along the trail.

How These Hikes Were Chosen

The hikes were picked to be compatible with the abilities of a wide variety of hikers. Most of the hikes are in the easy and moderate categories, which generally meet the needs of most hikers. There are, however, a couple of challenging hikes to keep the aerobic animals among us happy, and some that are very easy to meet the needs of groups with young children and laid-back adults. There are also four hikes that are wheelchair accessible.

Selecting a Hike

The hikes in this book are rated as to difficulty.

- Very easy hikes are generally less than 0.5 mile long, nearly flat, and often paved or a boardwalk.

- Easy hikes may be up to 3 miles long and will have very little elevation gain or loss.

- Moderate hikes can be several miles long and may have up to 750 feet of elevation gain and/or loss. The grades of moderate hikes are mostly gentle. Most hikers in relatively good condition will have no trouble with these hikes.

- Hikes rated challenging may have sections of steep, narrow, rough, and rocky trail. They are generally longer, over 9 miles in one case, and may have an elevation gain of 2,000 feet. None of these hikes will be difficult for a person in good physical condition, but they may be grueling for those people who are not.

The hiking times given are for hikers in fairly good physical condition. Hiking times do not include time spent sightseeing or picnicking. If there are children along, the hiking times should be increased to allow for the inspection of bugs, flowers, and other interesting things along the trail.

Trail Mileage

Trail mileage is mostly derived from the use of a GPS receiver. The mileages in the Miles and Directions section are rounded to the closest tenth mile. This may cause some discrepancy when reaching the total mileage for a hike. For instance, if the turnaround point is at 1.34 miles, it will be rounded to 1.3 miles. At the end of the hike the one-way distance would be doubled to 2.68 miles, which would be rounded to 2.7 miles.

Trail Finder

Best hikes for lake and pond lovers

1   Pine Lakes Loop
2   30 Acre Lake
3   Blackhorse Lake Boardwalk

Best hikes for river lovers

6   Deep Creek Overlook Loop
8   Bowl and Pitcher Loop
15   Blackwell Island Wetland Trail

Best hikes for nature lovers

1   Pine Lakes Loop
2   30 Acre Lake
3   Blackhorse Lake Boardwalk
4   Stubblefield Lake Loop
15   Blackwell Island Wetland Trail

Best hikes for history buffs

18   Mineral Ridge National Recreation Trail
19   Lost Man Trail
22   Mullan Military Road Interpretive Trail

Best hikes for great views

6   Deep Creek Overlook Loop
7   Deep Creek Bench Loop
8   Bowl and Pitcher Loop
11   Bald Knob–CCC Cabin
12   Mount Kit Carson
13   Mount Spokane Summit–Saddle Junction
14   Liberty Creek Loop
18   Mineral Ridge National Recreation Trail

Map Legend

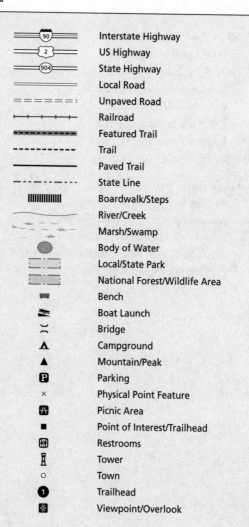

═══〈90〉═══	Interstate Highway
───〈2〉───	US Highway
───〈904〉───	State Highway
──────────	Local Road
==========	Unpaved Road
┣━┿━┿━┿━┫	Railroad
■■■■■■■■■■	Featured Trail
----------	Trail
──────────	Paved Trail
─·─·─·─·─	State Line
‖‖‖‖‖‖‖‖‖‖	Boardwalk/Steps
～～～	River/Creek
～～～	Marsh/Swamp
●	Body of Water
▭	Local/State Park
▭	National Forest/Wildlife Area
▬	Bench
⛵	Boat Launch
⌣	Bridge
Ⓐ	Campground
▲	Mountain/Peak
🅿	Parking
×	Physical Point Feature
🛆	Picnic Area
■	Point of Interest/Trailhead
🚻	Restrooms
🛆	Tower
○	Town
❶	Trailhead
🔭	Viewpoint/Overlook

1 Pine Lakes Loop

The Pine Lakes Loop Trail is an easy hike in the Turnbull National Wildlife Refuge. The route generally follows the shoreline of one of the Pine Lakes, offering an excellent opportunity to view several species of waterfowl. Moose are also occasionally seen here.

Distance: 1.2-mile lollipop loop
Hiking time: About 45 minutes
Difficulty: Easy
Trail surface: Wide paved trail
Best seasons: Year-round, weather permitting
Other trail users: Hikers only. This trail is wheelchair accessible.
Canine compatibility: Dogs are discouraged on the refuge; however, they are permitted as long as they are on a leash less than 5 feet long.
Fees and permits: A daily or annual Refuge Pass is required Mar through Oct; no fee is charged Nov through Feb. Several federal passes, including a Federal Duck Stamp, allow you to get on the refuge free. Daily Refuge Passes are self-purchased at the entrance to the refuge; annual passes must be obtained at the refuge headquarters.
Schedule: Daylight hours 7 days a week
Maps: The Turnbull National Wildlife Refuge brochure map is adequate for the hikes in the refuge, or just use the one in this book.
Trail contact: Turnbull National Wildlife Refuge, 26010 South Smith Rd., Cheney, WA 99004; (509) 235-4723; www.fws.gov/turnbull

Finding the trailhead: From downtown Spokane take I-90 west for 11 miles to exit 270. Take the exit and drive south for 6 miles on SR 904 to Cheney. Near the west end of Cheney, turn left (south) on the Cheney-Plaza Road and head south for 4 miles to the entrance road for the refuge (South Smith Road). Turn left and follow the signs toward the refuge headquarters. Just after leaving the Cheney-Plaza

Road, there will be a reader board and pay station on the right, where you can obtain your Refuge Pass. With your pass in hand, drive 3.3 miles to the Pine Lakes Trailhead. The elevation at the trailhead is 2,240 feet. GPS: N47 24.891'/W117 32.283'

The Hike

Cross the road from the parking area and pass a viewing area complete with binoculars, then wind your way down the short distance to near lake level. The track turns right (southwest) at the bottom of the hill. The marshy lake on your left is Winslow Pool. In 0.2 mile there will be a trail junction. Bear right (nearly straight ahead) and walk a short distance to another junction, which is the beginning of the loop portion of this hike.

Bear left (nearly straight ahead again) at the junction and hike north slightly back from the lakeshore, through the aspens and ponderosa pines. The route reaches Ice Pond Viewpoint 0.2 mile after passing the junction with the connector trail to the Stubblefield Lake Loop. There is a bench next to the trail just before reaching the viewpoint, and California quail are often present in the nearby brush.

Soon you will pass another reader board, also about the waterfowl. The course crosses an earthen dam 0.1 mile farther along. This dam divides Winslow Pool, which is on the right, and north Pine Lake on the left. Just across the dam there will be two trail junctions in quick succession. Stay on the main trail by bearing left at the first one, then turning right at the second. This completes the loop, so retrace your incoming steps for the 0.3 mile back to the trailhead.

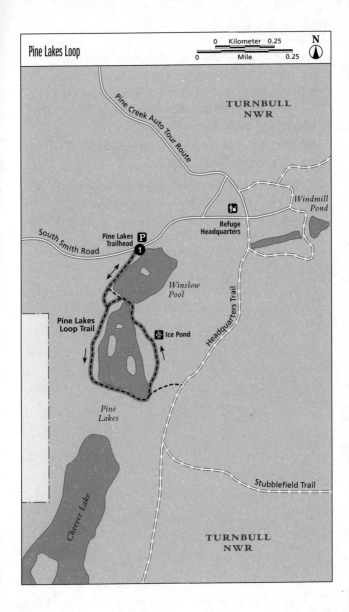

Pine Lakes Loop

0   Kilometer   0.25
0   Mile   0.25

N

TURNBULL
NWR

Pine Creek Auto Tour Route

Windmill
Pond

Refuge
Headquarters

South Smith Road

Pine Lakes
Trailhead

P

1

Winslow
Pool

Pine Lakes
Loop Trail

Ice Pond

Headquarters Trail

Pine
Lakes

Cheever Lake

Stubblefield Trail

TURNBULL
NWR

Miles and Directions

0.0 Begin your hike from the Pine Lakes Trailhead.

0.3 Bear right at the second trail junction to begin the loop.

0.5 Pass the trail junction with the path that connects to the Stubblefield Lake Loop. Bear left, staying on the main trail.

0.7 Stop for a moment at the Ice Pond Viewpoint.

0.9 Turn right at the trail junction, ending the loop.

1.2 Return to the Pine Lakes Trailhead.

Options: There are other short hikes along the Pine Creek Auto Tour Route. For a longer trip, take the Stubble-field Lake Loop (Hike 4), which can be accessed via the Pine Lakes Loop or from the refuge headquarters.

2 30 Acre Lake

This is a fairly short, easy, and somewhat out-of-the-way hike on the Turnbull National Wildlife Refuge. Hiking this route offers excellent wildlife-viewing possibilities.

Distance: 1.6 miles out and back
Hiking time: About 1 hour
Difficulty: Easy
Trail surface: Dirt service road
Best seasons: Year-round, weather permitting
Other trail users: Hikers only
Canine compatibility: Dogs are discouraged on the refuge; however, they are permitted as long as they are on a leash less than 5 feet long.
Fees and permits: A daily or annual Refuge Pass is required Mar through Oct; no fee is charged Nov through Feb. Several federal passes, including a Federal Duck Stamp, allow you to get on the refuge free. Daily Refuge Passes are self-purchased at the entrance to the refuge; annual passes must be obtained at the refuge headquarters.
Schedule: Daylight hours 7 days a week
Maps: The Turnbull National Wildlife Refuge brochure map is adequate for the hikes in the refuge, or just use the one in this book.
Trail contact: Turnbull National Wildlife Refuge, 26010 South Smith Rd., Cheney, WA 99004; (509) 235-4723; www.fws.gov/turnbull

Finding the trailhead: From downtown Spokane take I-90 west for 11 miles to exit 270. Take the exit and drive south for 6 miles on SR 904 to Cheney. Near the west end of Cheney, turn left (south) on the Cheney-Plaza Road and head south for 4 miles to the entrance road for the Turnbull National Wildlife Refuge (South Smith Road). Turn left and follow the signs toward the refuge headquarters. Just after leaving the Cheney-Plaza Road, there will be a reader board and pay station on the right, where you can obtain your refuge pass. Drive

3.5 miles to the entrance for the Pine Creek Auto Tour Route (you will pass the tour route exit before you reach the entrance). Turn left on the tour route and go 1.1 miles north to the south 30 Acre Lake Trailhead and Parking Area. Only limited parking and no other facilities are available at the south trailhead. GPS: N47 25.681'/W117 32.279'

The north trailhead, which is 2.1 miles farther along the tour route, also has only limited parking and no other facilities. GPS: N47 26.226'/W 117 32.494'

The Hike

The best time to take this hike is in the early morning in September, when the rutting elk will be bugling, their high-pitched voices challenging each other for dominance. Really, an early morning at any time of the year is a great time to take this hike. Vociferous coyotes may be making themselves heard, and other wildlife is often seen. Moose are sometimes spotted along this route. For safety, watch moose from a distance and don't challenge them in any way.

From the parking area, begin your hike by heading north-northwest on the dirt service road. In a little less than 0.2 mile there will be a sign marking 30 Acre Lake. Take a minute here to look for waterfowl that may be cruising the lake surface. The track crosses a marsh and a small creek that may be dry, then passes a grove of aspen trees. Before long the tread passes the north end of another marsh and climbs a few feet. You then continue northwest, through open ponderosa pine forest, to the junction with the tour route at the north trailhead. Unless you have arranged for there to be a vehicle at this trailhead, this is your turnaround point, so retrace your steps back to the south trailhead.

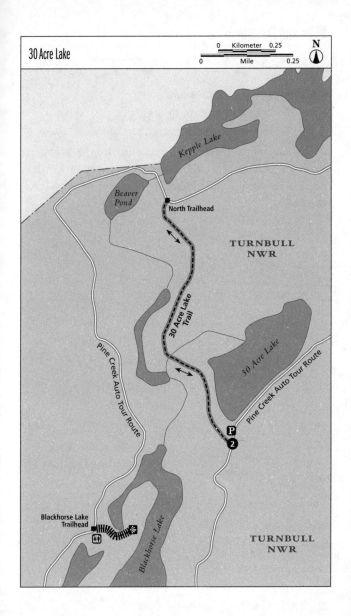

30 Acre Lake

Kepple Lake

Beaver Pond

North Trailhead

TURNBULL NWR

30 Acre Lake Trail

30 Acre Lake

Pine Creek Auto Tour Route

Pine Creek Auto Tour Route

P
2

Blackhorse Lake Trailhead

Blackhorse Lake

TURNBULL NWR

N

Kilometer
0   0.25

Mile
0   0.25

Miles and Directions

0.0 Hike north-northwest from the south trailhead and parking area.

0.2 Pass the 30 Acre Lake sign.

0.8 Turn around at the north trailhead.

1.6 Return to the south trailhead and parking area.

Option: Since the Pine Creek Auto Tour is a one-way road, you may want to stop and walk the very short Blackhorse Lake Boardwalk (Hike 3) on the same trip. It's on your way.

3 Blackhorse Lake Boardwalk

The Blackhorse Lake Boardwalk is a very short, easy stroll on the Turnbull National Wildlife Refuge. The trail leads to a platform viewpoint overlooking Blackhorse Lake and the wetlands that surround it.

Distance: 0.2 mile out and back

Hiking time: About 10 minutes, plus the time you take to sit and watch the birds

Difficulty: Very easy

Trail surface: Paved trail and boardwalk

Best seasons: Year-round, weather permitting

Other trail users: Hikers only. This trail is wheelchair accessible.

Canine compatibility: Dogs are discouraged on the refuge; however, they are permitted as long as they are on a leash less than 5 feet long.

Fees and permits: A daily or annual Refuge Pass is required Mar through Oct; no fee is charged Nov through Feb. Several federal passes, including a Federal Duck Stamp, allow you to get on the refuge free. Daily Refuge Passes are self-purchased at the entrance to the refuge; annual passes must be obtained at the refuge headquarters.

Schedule: Daylight hours 7 days a week

Maps: The Turnbull National Wildlife Refuge brochure map is adequate for the hikes in the refuge, or just use the one in this book.

Trail contact: Turnbull National Wildlife Refuge, 26010 South Smith Rd., Cheney, WA 99004; (509) 235-4723; www.fws.gov/turnbull

Finding the trailhead: From downtown Spokane drive west on I-90 for 11 miles to exit 270. Take the exit and drive south for 6 miles on SR 904 to Cheney. Near the west end of Cheney, turn left (south) on the Cheney-Plaza Road; a sign here points to the Turnbull

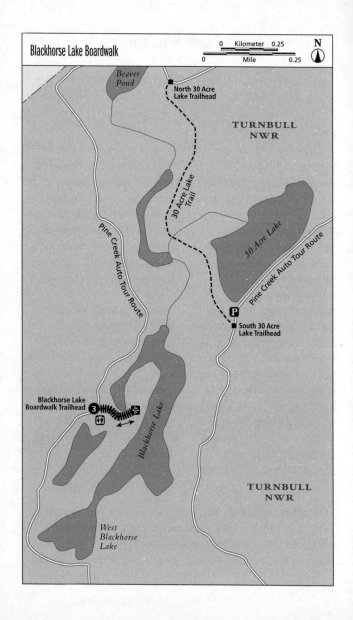

Blackhorse Lake Boardwalk

0   Kilometer   0.25
0   Mile   0.25

N

Beaver
Pond

North 30 Acre
Lake Trailhead

TURNBULL
NWR

30 Acre Lake Trail

30 Acre Lake

Pine Creek Auto Tour Route

Pine Creek Auto Tour Route

P

South 30 Acre
Lake Trailhead

Blackhorse Lake
Boardwalk Trailhead

3

Blackhorse Lake

West
Blackhorse
Lake

TURNBULL
NWR

Refuge. Head south for 4 miles to the entrance road for the refuge (South Smith Road) and turn left. Just after leaving the Cheney-Plaza Road, there will be a reader board and pay station on the right, where you can obtain your refuge pass. Drive 3.5 miles to the entrance for the Pine Creek Auto Tour Route (you will pass the auto tour route exit before you reach the entrance). Turn left on the tour route and go 4.6 miles to the Blackhorse Lake Boardwalk Trailhead. There is adequate parking and restrooms at the trailhead. GPS: N47 25.480'/W117 32.728'

The Hike

Walk east from the parking area on the paved trail, which in a very short distance becomes a boardwalk. A few steps farther along, stop and read the reader board. The boardwalk soon ends, and a few steps more bring you to the Blackhorse Lake Viewing Platform. Benches on the platform make it a great place to sit quietly and watch the waterfowl as well as the other species of birds that inhabit these wetlands. Blackbirds are common here, and California quail are often seen or heard. When you are ready, return as you came.

Miles and Directions

0.0 Hike east from the Blackhorse Lake Boardwalk Trailhead.
0.1 Sit quietly and enjoy the wildlife at the Blackhorse Lake Viewing Platform.
0.2 Return to the Blackhorse Lake Boardwalk Trailhead.

4 Stubblefield Lake Loop

The Stubblefield Lake Loop provides a good overall cross section of the types of terrain that can be found on the Turnbull Refuge. The trail starts in semi-open ponderosa pine timberland then breaks out into open grassland, providing the hiker with an introduction to the types of habitat available here. Watch for coyotes, deer, and elk in the upland areas as well as waterfowl on the lakes and possible moose along the shorelines.

Distance: 5.6-mile lollipop loop

Hiking time: About 2.5 hours

Difficulty: Moderate, mostly because of the distance

Trail surface: Gravel and dirt service roads

Best seasons: Year-round, weather permitting

Other trail users: Hikers only

Canine compatibility: Dogs are discouraged on the refuge; however, they are permitted as long as they are on a leash less than 5 feet long.

Fees and permits: A daily or annual Refuge Pass is required Mar through Oct; no fee is charged Nov through Feb. Several federal passes, including a Federal Duck Stamp, allow you to get on the refuge free. Daily Refuge Passes are self-purchased at the entrance to the refuge; annual passes must be obtained at the refuge headquarters.

Schedule: Daylight hours 7 days a week

Maps: The Turnbull National Wildlife Refuge brochure map is adequate for the hikes in the refuge, or just use the one in this book. The National Geographic Washington topo on CD-ROM Disk 4 shows very well the service roads that make up this hike.

Trail contact: Turnbull National Wildlife Refuge, 26010 South Smith Rd., Cheney, WA 99004; (509) 235-4723; www.fws.gov/turnbull

Special considerations: Much of this route is without shade and may be very hot during the summer.

Finding the trailhead: From downtown Spokane drive west on I-90 for 11 miles to exit 270. Take the exit and drive south for 6 miles on SR 904 to Cheney. Near the west end of Cheney, turn left (south) on the Cheney-Plaza Road and head south for 4 miles to the entrance road for the refuge (South Smith Road). Turn left and follow the signs to the Turnbull National Wildlife Refuge Headquarters and Trailhead. Just after leaving the Cheney-Plaza Road, there will be a reader board and pay station on the right, where you can obtain your refuge pass. There is parking for several cars and a visitor center at the refuge headquarters and trailhead. GPS: N47 24.931'/W117 31.900'

The Hike

There are no signs at the refuge headquarters to mark the spot where this hike starts. Park in the parking area and walk to the east, around the left side of a building. At the east end of the building, a gravel service road leads south (right). This road is the starting point for the Stubblefield Lake Loop hike. The road is normally blocked to close it to all but authorized (refuge personnel) vehicle traffic. Walk around the barricade and begin your hike to the south along the service road.

In a short distance you will arrive at a junction. The road to the left leads to an environmental education shelter and Headquarters Pond. Keep right and soon climb gently through the open ponderosa pine woods. There will be another junction 0.5 mile into the hike. The route to the right is a short connector trail between this loop and the Pine Lakes Loop to the west. Hike straight ahead (south) for 0.2 mile to another junction and the beginning point of the loop portion of this hike. Before reaching the junction, you will have a good view to the right of Pine Lakes as you hike across the grassland surrounded by pine trees. Continue to hike straight ahead (south) at this junction.

In the next 0.7 mile the route descends slightly and reenters the timber close to the southern end of Cheever Lake, the most southern of the Pine Lakes, where there is another junction. When I hiked through here, the willows to the right of the route near this junction were heavily browsed to moose height. Keep a watch for one of these huge animals, and if you see one, don't approach or challenge it in any way. Some moose have a poor attitude, and all of them are unpredictable and potentially dangerous. As with all wildlife, getting too close is not the thing to do.

Turn left at the junction and climb very gently to the southeast through the pine woods. There will be another road to the right shortly after leaving the junction. Bear left here, staying on the main roadbed, which is now mostly dirt surfaced instead of gravel.

The track leaves the timber 0.8 mile past the junction at the south end of Pine Lakes. You hike southeast across the grassland for 0.4 mile, then turn east along a fence line, which is the southern boundary of the Turnbull Refuge. After following the fence for almost 0.3 mile, the route turns northeast, leaving the fence line and the poor road beside it.

Another 0.6 mile of hiking brings you to the junction next to Stubblefield Lake. This route reaches its highest point, about 2,360 feet, between the fence line and the junction near the lake. The lakebed, which is to the right, is important habitat for migrating waterfowl and shorebirds. The lake itself is small or almost nonexistent, depending on the season. Turn left at the junction next to Stubblefield Lake and hike to the northwest, across the grassland. Small

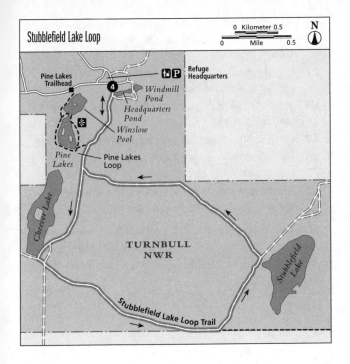

Stubblefield Lake Loop

Pine Lakes Trailhead

Refuge Headquarters

Windmill Pond

Headquarters Pond

Winslow Pool

Pine Lakes

Pine Lakes Loop

Cheever Lake

TURNBULL NWR

Stubblefield Lake

Stubblefield Lake Loop Trail

groves of aspens stud the rolling prairie. If you're here morning or evening, watch for elk in this semi-open country.

About 0.7 mile after leaving Stubblefield Lake, the track passes between a small pond and a marsh. The tread turns west after another 0.1 mile. You then climb over a small rise and reach the junction that ends the loop, 0.8 mile after heading west. Turn right at this junction and retrace your steps to the refuge headquarters and the end of this hike.

Miles and Directions

0.0   Leave the refuge headquarters and trailhead, hiking south.

0.5 Hike straight ahead (south), then bear left (straight ahead) at the trail (road) junction with the connector to Pine Lakes Loop.

0.7 Hike straight ahead (south). Bear right at the trail (road) junction to begin the loop.

1.4 Reach the trail (road) junction at the south end of Cheever Lake and turn left.

2.9 At the trail (road) junction, bear left, leaving the fence line.

3.4 Turn left and hike northwest from the trail (road) junction next to Stubblefield Lake.

4.9 Reach the junction at the end of the loop and turn right.

5.6 Return to the refuge headquarters and trailhead.

Option: Combine this hike with the Pine Lakes Loop (Hike 1) via the connector trail that is 0.5 mile from the Refuge Headquarters Trailhead (also 0.5 mile from the Pine Lakes Trailhead).

5 Columbia Plateau Trail

The Columbia Plateau Trail is a Rails to Trails project. The portion of the trail described here is paved and, being so close to Cheney, receives considerable bicycle traffic. This is a great route to hike with children, especially kids who like trains, as it is likely that you will get a close look at one on a parallel track or overhead bridge crossing. Muskrats may sometimes be seen in the sluggish streams that parallel the route in places. If a car shuttle can be arranged to the Fish Lake Trailhead, this hike can be made one way, cutting the total distance in half.

Distance: 7.7 miles out and back

Hiking time: About 3 hours

Difficulty: Nearly flat grade; moderate only because of length

Trail surface: Wide paved trail

Best seasons: Year-round, snow conditions permitting

Other trail users: Bicyclists are the most common users of this trail. Horses are prohibited on the section of trail described here, but are permitted on the unpaved section to the south-west. This portion of the Columbia Plateau Trail is wheelchair accessible.

Canine compatibility: Dogs MUST be leashed. This is very important because of the large number of bicycles on this trail.

Fees and permits: Discover Pass, available where fishing licenses are sold

Schedule: Summer 6:30 a.m. to dusk, winter 8 a.m. to dusk

Maps: The map included here is more than adequate for this hike. The National Geographic Washington topo on CD-ROM Disk 4 covers the area very well but shows this route as a railroad track (which it once was), as do many other maps.

Trail contact: At present this section of the Columbia Plateau Trail is managed by Riverside State Park, 9711 West Charles Rd., Nine Mile Falls, WA 99026; (509) 465-5064; www.riverside statepark.org.

Finding the trailhead: From downtown Spokane take I-90 west for 11 miles to exit 270. Take the exit and drive south for 6 miles on SR 904 to Cheney. From Cheney drive south 1 mile from SR 904 on the Cheney-Spangle Road. The parking area and trailhead are on the left side of the road. Restrooms and shaded picnic tables are available at the trailhead, but no water. The elevation at the trailhead is 2,300 feet. GPS: N47 28.767'/W117 33.652'

The Hike

The hike begins at the northwest corner of the parking area. Descend the paved path for a few yards to the Columbia Plateau Trail and turn right. Here a trail sign informs you that it is 0.25 mile to the water station and 3.75 miles to Fish Lake Trailhead. In both cases the actual distances are slightly farther. Other signs state that the maximum speed is 15 mph (for bicycles) and that you are entering the city of Cheney. The trail follows the old railroad grade to the northwest, through a cut. Aspen and ponderosa pine trees line the rim of the cut. The route passes Mile Marker 361 0.3 mile from the trailhead. In another 0.1 mile you reach the water station, which is on the left. There is a fountain here, along with shade and a bench. At the water station the route enters a more open area.

The broad, paved tread traverses the open country for 0.2 mile, then the trees show up again as the course passes through a cut in the layered basalt. A sluggish stream follows the grade through the cut. One and one-tenth mile from the trailhead the course leaves the city of Cheney and shortly passes Mile Marker 362. Soon the route passes beneath a railroad overpass, then goes beneath a wooden bridge 0.2 mile farther along.

About 2 miles from the trailhead the route leaves the cut. To the left of the trail is a field and a house, and to the

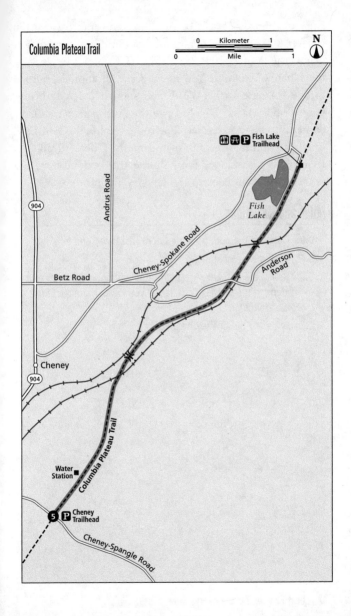

Columbia Plateau Trail

0   Kilometer   1

0   Mile   1

N

904

Andrus Road

Fish Lake Trailhead

Fish Lake

Cheney-Spokane Road

Anderson Road

Betz Road

Cheney

904

Columbia Plateau Trail

Water Station

5 P Cheney Trailhead

Cheney-Spangle Road

right is a railroad track. Before long the route passes Mile Marker 363 and soon enters another cut. The course passes below the Anderson Road Bridge 2.7 miles after leaving the Cheney Trailhead. You go underneath another railroad bridge 0.4 mile farther along, and another 0.2 mile brings you to Mile Marker 364. Just past the mile marker Fish Lake comes into view to the left. The route reaches the Fish Lake Trailhead slightly over 3.8 miles from the Cheney Trailhead. If you haven't arranged a car shuttle, turn around here and retrace your steps back to the Cheney Trailhead.

Miles and Directions

0.0 Descend the path from the Cheney Trailhead and turn right.

0.4 Pass the water station.

3.8 Reach the Fish Lake Trailhead. Turn around and retrace your steps to the Cheney Trailhead (if you haven't arranged for a car shuttle).

7.7 Return to the Cheney Trailhead.

6 Deep Creek Overlook Loop

The Deep Creek Overlook Loop hike is interesting geologically as well as very scenic. Allow longer than you generally would for a 2.4-mile hike so you can take the time to enjoy these features.

Distance: 2.4-mile lollipop loop
Hiking time: About 1.5 hours
Difficulty: Moderate, with a couple of challenging spots
Trail surface: Dirt singletrack, broad paved trail, and gravel road (closed to unauthorized motor vehicles)
Best seasons: Spring, summer, and fall; also winter if there's no snow cover
Other trail users: Bicycles are also allowed and are the most common traffic on the Centennial Trail portion of this loop.
Canine compatibility: Dogs are permitted on a leash.

Fees and permits: Discover Pass, available where fishing licenses are sold
Schedule: Summer 6:30 a.m. to dusk, winter 8 a.m. to dusk
Map: *Riverside State Park Multi-use Trails Map,* produced by the Inland Empire Backcountry Horsemen, PO Box 30891, Spokane, WA 99223; www.iebch .com. This map may be purchased at the state park.
Trail contact: Riverside State Park, 9711 West Charles Rd., Nine Mile Falls, WA 99026; (509) 465-5064; www.riverside statepark.org

Finding the trailhead: There are many ways to reach this trailhead; this is a route from the center of Spokane. Take Division Street north from I-90 to Francis, which is SR 291. Turn left on Francis and follow it west to 9-Mile Road, which is also SR 291. Bear right on 9-Mile Road and drive northwest for 2 miles to 7-Mile Road. Turn left on 7-Mile Road and head west for 2.1 miles to State Park Drive. Turn right on State Park Drive and go 0.4 mile to the locked gate. The wide spot just before reaching the gate is the trailhead parking area. There are no other facilities at the trailhead. This trailhead, at 1,820 feet elevation, is also used as an entrance and exit point for the Centennial Trail. GPS: N47 45.242' / W117 32.926'

The Hike

Follow the road (a continuation of State Park Drive) north from the trailhead, passing the gate. In 0.2 mile the 25-Mile Trail crosses the road. Turn left on the 25-Mile Trail and start the loop part of this hike by descending into Deep Creek Canyon. There are really two trails here descending into the canyon. Try to follow the one that is marked with the 25-MILE trail markers. These trails meet just before reaching the canyon bottom. The trail loses about 50 feet of elevation by the time you reach the bottom.

After the short but steep descent to the creek bed, the route turns right. Head down the creek bed for a few feet, then turn left and begin the climb out of the west side of the canyon. The track climbs steeply, making a couple of switchbacks, before reaching the junction with Trail 411. This junction is 0.6 mile from the Deep Creek Trailhead at 1,780 feet elevation.

Turn right at the junction and follow Trail 411. The course now traverses an area of large lava rock outcrops and talus slopes. This area is directly across Deep Creek Canyon from the Deep Creek Overlook, which you will pass farther along on this loop. Before long the trail starts to descend, and you make a couple of steep, rocky switchbacks before reaching the junction with the Centennial Trail. This junction is 1.2 miles from the trailhead, at 1,620 feet elevation.

Turn right on the broad, paved Centennial Trail and head east. The route quickly crosses a bridge and begins to climb very gently. To the left is the Spokane River, or more

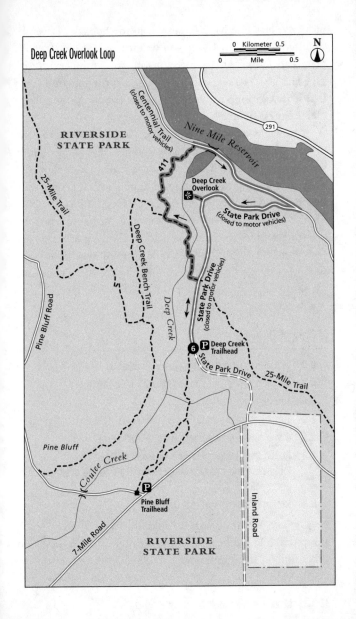

Deep Creek Overlook Loop

0   Kilometer   0.5

0   Mile   0.5

N

RIVERSIDE
STATE PARK

Centennial Trail
(closed to motor vehicles)

Nine Mile Reservoir

291

411

Deep Creek
Overlook

25-Mile Trail

State Park Drive
(closed to motor vehicles)

Deep Creek Bench Trail

Pine Bluff Road

Deep Creek

State Park Drive
(closed to motor vehicles)

6   Deep Creek
Trailhead

State Park Drive

25-Mile Trail

Pine Bluff

Coulee Creek

Pine Bluff
Trailhead

Inland Road

7-Mile Road

RIVERSIDE
STATE PARK

properly the Nine Mile Reservoir in the Spokane River. In slightly more than 0.4 mile you will reach the junction with State Park Drive. At this junction you are 1.6 miles into the hike and at 1,710 feet elevation. A sign at the junction states that it is 0.25 mile to Deep Creek Overlook and 1 mile to Deep Creek Trailhead.

Turn right on State Park Drive, which is closed to unauthorized motor vehicles, and continue the gentle climb, soon passing a gate. There will be a trail to the right 0.3 mile after leaving the Centennial Trail. Turn right and walk the short distance to the Deep Creek Overlook (GPS: N47 45.671'/W117 32.928'). After savoring the view from the overlook, and maybe having a snack, walk back to State Park Drive and turn right. In 0.25 mile you will reach the junction with the 25-Mile Trail, completing the loop. Continue on the roadway for another 0.2 mile to the Deep Creek Trailhead, where this hike started.

Miles and Directions

0.0 Hike north from the Deep Creek Trailhead.

0.2 Turn left at the junction with the 25-Mile Trail.

0.6 Turn right on Trail 411.

1.2 Turn right on the wide, paved Centennial Trail.

1.6 Climb to the right (west) on State Park Drive.

1.9 Reach the junction with the side trail to Deep Creek Overlook. Walk the short distance to the right, to the overlook and back.

2.4 Return to the Deep Creek Trailhead.

Option: You may want to hike the Deep Creek Bench Loop (Hike 7) on the same trip. A small portion of these two hikes follows the same route.

7 Deep Creek Bench Loop

Hike the open forests on the benches above Deep Creek and Coulee Creek Canyons. This geologically interesting hike combines several different trails, keeping the hiker on his or her toes at the many junctions.

Distance: 2.9-mile loop
Hiking time: About 2 hours
Difficulty: Moderate, with a few short but challenging spots
Trail surface: Dirt singletracks and gravel roads
Best seasons: Spring, summer, fall; winter if there's no snow cover
Other trail users: Equestrians and mountain bikers. The Pine Bluff Trailhead is a designated equestrian trailhead.
Canine compatibility: Dogs are permitted on a leash.
Fees and permits: Discover Pass, available where fishing licenses are sold
Schedule: Summer 6 a.m. to dusk, winter 8 a.m. to dusk

Map: *Riverside State Park Multi-use Trails Map,* produced by the Inland Empire Backcountry Horsemen, PO Box 30891, Spokane, WA 99223; www.iebch .com. This map may be purchased at the state park.
Trail contact: Riverside State Park, 9711 West Charles Rd., Nine Mile Falls, WA 99026; (509) 465-5064; www.riverside statepark.org
Special considerations: The hike description below may seem complicated due to the many trail junctions on this route. Watch the map closely as you hike, and the directions will become much simpler.

Finding the trailhead: There are many ways to reach this trailhead; this is a route from the center of Spokane. Take Division Street north from I-90 to Francis, which is SR 291. Turn left on Francis and follow it to 9-Mile Road, which is also SR 291. Bear right on 9-Mile Road and drive northwest for 2 miles to 7-Mile Road. Turn left on 7-Mile Road and head west for 2.5 miles to the Pine Bluff Trailhead at the junction with Pine Bluff Road. The trailhead and parking area are on the right side of 7-Mile Road. There is adequate parking but no restrooms at the Pine Bluff Trailhead. The elevation at the trailhead is 1,840 feet. GPS: N47 44.864' / W117 33.152'

The Hike

Hike northeast from the trailhead on the dirt road (not open to motor vehicles). A few yards of traveling through the open ponderosa pine forest will bring you to a junction. There are no signs here. Bear right and continue to traverse the open woods to the northeast. In another 0.3 mile the roadbeds rejoin each other. At this point leave the roadbed, head north on the singletrack, and descend for about 100 yards into the small canyon. The route reaches the creek bed at the bottom of the canyon, very close to the point where Coulee Creek joins Deep Creek. Both of these creeks may well be dry. The trail crosses the creek bed, then climbs north for a little less than 0.2 mile to the Deep Creek Trailhead on State Park Drive. The trailhead is just a wide spot in the road at 1,820 feet elevation.

Head north from the trailhead, following the road (a continuation of State Park Drive) and passing a gate. In 0.2 mile turn left on the 25-Mile Trail and start the descent into Deep Creek Canyon. There are really two trails here descending into the canyon. Try to follow the one that is marked with the 25-MILE trail markers. These trails meet just before reaching the canyon bottom. The route loses about 50 feet of elevation by the time you reach the bottom.

After the short but steep descent to the creek bed, the course turns right. Head down the creek bed for a few feet, then turn left and begin the climb out of the west side of the canyon. The track climbs steeply, making a couple of switchbacks, before reaching the junction with Trail 411. This junction is 1.2 miles from the Pine Bluff Trailhead at 1,780 feet elevation.

Turn left at the junction, staying on the 25-Mile Trail. The course climbs for 0.25 mile to another junction. Turn left here, leaving the 25-Mile Trail, and climb, making six switchbacks in the 0.1 mile to the junction with Trail 410. Bear left (nearly straight ahead) on Trail 410 and hike generally south. The track follows a bench, climbing slightly for 0.25 mile before flattening out at about 1,950 feet elevation. The route continues south on the bench, through ponderosa pine and Douglas fir forest, to another junction. This Y junction, 1.8 miles into this loop, is with the 25-Mile Trail again.

Bear left at the junction and hike south on the 25-Mile Trail. The route descends a little, then flattens out again on the bench. Four-tenths mile from the junction, the course gets close to the rim of Coulee Creek Canyon. The canyon is to the left; above to the right are rugged rock cliffs. After traversing the bench for 0.6 mile, the trail descends the last few yards to the junction with Pine Bluff Road. This junction 2.5 miles into the loop is at 1,910 feet elevation. Turn left on Pine Bluff Road and hike the 0.4 mile back to the Pine Bluff Trailhead.

Miles and Directions

0.0 Hike northeast from the Pine Bluff Trailhead.

0.5 Head north along State Park Drive from the Deep Creek Trailhead.

0.7 Turn left on the 25-Mile Trail.

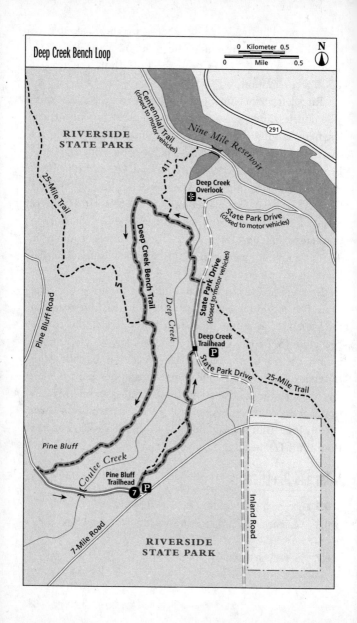

Deep Creek Bench Loop

RIVERSIDE
STATE PARK

Nine Mile Reservoir

Centennial Trail
(closed to motor vehicles)

411

25-Mile Trail

Deep Creek
Overlook

State Park Drive
(closed to motor vehicles)

Deep Creek Bench Trail

Deep Creek

State Park Drive
(closed to motor vehicles)

Deep Creek
Trailhead
P

State Park Drive

25-Mile Trail

Pine Bluff Road

Pine Bluff

Coulee Creek

Pine Bluff
Trailhead
7 P

7-Mile Road

Inland Road

RIVERSIDE
STATE PARK

N

0   Kilometer   0.5
0   Mile   0.5

1.2 Turn left, staying on the 25-Mile Trail at the junction with Trail 411.

1.4 Turn left at the junction with Trail 410.

1.8 Bear left at the junction with the 25-Mile Trail.

2.5 The trail intersects Pine Bluff Road. Turn left and hike southeast on the road.

2.9 Return to the Pine Bluff Trailhead.

Option: Hike the Deep Creek Overlook Loop (Hike 6) on the same trip.

8 Bowl and Pitcher Loop

The first half of the Bowl and Pitcher Loop closely follows the bank of the beautiful Spokane River. You then return on a broad trail through mixed conifer forest to the Swinging Bridge Trailhead.

Distance: 2-mile lollipop loop

Hiking time: About 1 hour

Difficulty: Easy

Trail surface: Dirt singletrack and roadbed

Best seasons: Spring, summer, fall; winter if there's no snow cover

Other trail users: Bicyclists

Canine compatibility: Dogs are permitted on a leash.

Fees and permits: Discover Pass, available where fishing licenses are sold

Schedule: Summer 6:30 a.m. to dusk, winter 8 a.m. to dusk

Maps: *Riverside State Park Multi-use Trails Map,* produced by the Inland Empire Backcountry Horsemen, PO Box 30891, Spokane, WA 99223; www.ie bch.com. This map may be purchased at the state park. The National Geographic Washington topo is on CD-ROM Disk 4.

Trail contact: Riverside State Park, 9711 Charles Rd., Nine Mile Falls, WA 99026; (509) 465-5064; www.riversidestate park.org

Finding the trailhead: There are many ways to reach this trailhead; this is a route from the center of Spokane. Take Division Street north from I-90 to Francis, which is SR 291. Turn west (left) on SR 291 and go 3.8 miles to the junction with Rifle Club Road. A sign here points to the Bowl and Pitcher area. Turn left on Rifle Club Road and drive 0.4 mile southwest to Aubrey L. White Parkway. Turn left on Aubrey L. White Parkway and drive 2 miles south to the Bowl and Pitcher area, which includes a campground and day-use area. The trailhead is on the west side of the area, at the east end of the Swinging Bridge. Signs point the way. There is plenty of parking, restrooms, and a campground close to the trailhead. The *Riverside State Park Multi-use Trails Map* may be helpful here. GPS: N47 41.801'/W117 29.818'

The Hike

Read the reader board at the east end of the Swinging Bridge, then cross the bridge and begin your hike. As you cross the bridge, the Bowl and Pitcher rock formation is to your right. After crossing the bridge the route climbs a few feet to the junction with the 25-Mile Trail. Turn right at the junction and pass a path to the picnic shelter, which is to the right.

The track threads its way through rock outcroppings as you hike north. Several poor paths leave the trail on both sides, but the main trail is broad and easy to follow. Three-tenths mile from the first junction, the 25-Mile Trail (which you are now on) reaches a junction with Trails 210 and 211. Turn right, staying on the 25-Mile Trail, and start the loop.

Shortly there will be another junction; bear left here (really straight ahead), staying on the main trail. Rapids in the Spokane River are in view below and to the right. Heading northeast, the tread follows the top of the river-bank, well above the clear rushing waters. The course goes beneath some power lines 0.6 mile from the trailhead. A quarter mile farther along you will come to an unmarked trail junction. Bear right, staying on the main trail along the riverbank. There is a view of rapids in the river with a column of rock, known as the Devil's Toe Nail, rising from the center of the frothing waters 0.3 mile farther along.

A few more yards of hiking brings you to Mile Marker 20. Just past the mile marker there will be another trail

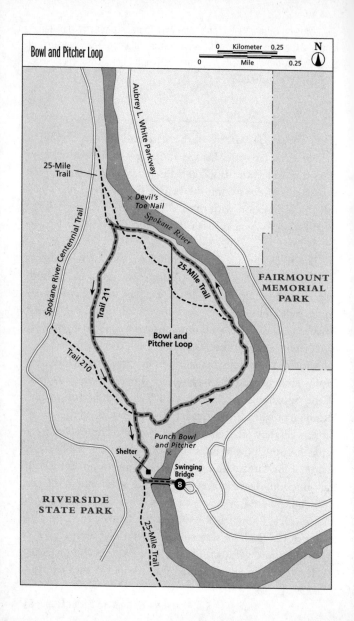

Bowl and Pitcher Loop

Kilometer 0.25
Mile 0.25

N

25-Mile Trail

Aubrey L. White Parkway

Devil's Toe Nail

Spokane River

Spokane River Centennial Trail

25-Mile Trail

FAIRMOUNT MEMORIAL PARK

Trail 211

Bowl and Pitcher Loop

Trail 210

Punch Bowl and Pitcher

Shelter

Swinging Bridge

8

RIVERSIDE STATE PARK

25-Mile Trail

junction. Turn left here, leaving the 25-Mile Trail, and climb a short distance west to yet another junction, this one with the abandoned roadbed, which is Trail 211. The trail, which turned left off the 25-Mile Trail 0.5 mile back, also rejoins the route (coming in from the southeast) at this junction. See the map for clarification here.

Turn left on the roadbed, which is Trail 211, and hike south. Rock outcroppings rise above the right side of the track 0.3 mile after leaving the junction. Another 0.2 mile of hiking will bring you to the junction with Trail 210 and the 25-Mile Trail, where the loop began. Hike straight ahead, retracing your steps to the Swinging Bridge, then cross the bridge to the trailhead.

Miles and Directions

0.0   Cross the Swinging Bridge as you leave the Swinging Bridge Trailhead.

0.4   Turn right at the junction with Trails 210 and 211, staying on the 25-Mile Trail and starting the loop.

1.1   Turn left on Trail 211 (roadbed), leaving the 25-Mile Trail.

1.6   Hike straight ahead at the junction with Trail 210 and the 25-Mile Trail, ending the loop.

2.0   Return to the Swinging Bridge Trailhead.

$\bigcirc$ 9   Entrance Loop

The Entrance Loop is a very pleasant hike through widely diverse second-growth forest. The route is wide all the way, never very steep, and has no cliffs close to it, making it an excellent hike for children.

Distance: 1.5-mile loop

Hiking time: About 1 hour

Difficulty: Moderate

Trail surface: Dirt roadbed (abandoned)

Best seasons: Late spring, summer, and fall for hiking. This is a great snowshoeing trail during the winter.

Other trail users: Open to bicyclists and equestrians during the summer season. In the winter snowshoers use the route. Snowmobiles may only use the Trail 120 section of this loop.

Canine compatibility: Pets must be on a leash and under physical control at all times.

Fees and permits: Discover Pass, available where fishing licenses are sold and online at www.discoverpass.wa.gov. A Snopark permit is required during the winter season.

Schedule: Summer 6:30 a.m. to dusk, winter 6:30 a.m. to 10 p.m.

Map: Mount Spokane State Park map, produced by Washington State Parks

Trail contact: Mount Spokane State Park, 26107 North Mount Spokane Park Dr., Mead, WA 99021; (509) 238-4258; www .parks.wa.gov

Finding the trailhead: From downtown Spokane head north on Division Street to the junction with US 2 (Newport Highway). Follow US 2 to the junction with SR 206 (Mount Spokane Park Drive). Turn right on SR 206 and drive 15.3 miles to the Mount Spokane State Park entrance. Pass the entrance and go another 0.3 mile to the Entrance Loop Trailhead. Parking and restrooms are on the left side of

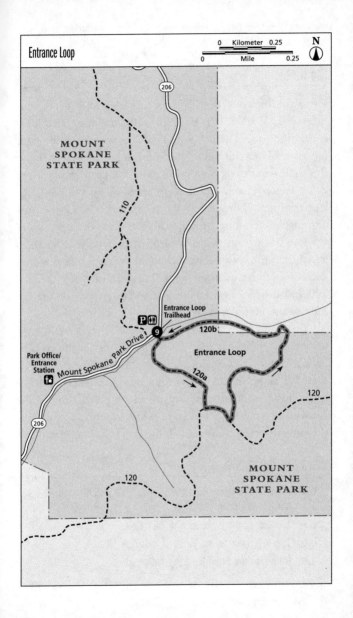

Entrance Loop

MOUNT
SPOKANE
STATE PARK

MOUNT
SPOKANE
STATE PARK

Park Office/
Entrance
Station

Entrance Loop
Trailhead

Entrance Loop

Mount Spokane Park Drive

110

120

120a

120b

120

206

206

N

Kilometer   0.25

Mile   0.25

the road. This hike begins across the road from the parking area, at 3,230 feet elevation. GPS: N47 53.292' / W117 07.510'

The Hike

Cross the highway from the parking area and begin your hike up Trail 120a. Two trails leave this trailhead; Trail 120a is the right one. The other trail is 120b, which will be your return trail on this hike. The route climbs moderately to the south-southwest as you leave the trailhead. Western red cedar, western larch, and western hemlock, as well as Douglas fir and grand fir, shadow the course, with Rocky Mountain maple providing an understory in the more open spots.

The track soon makes a turn to the left (southeast). In about 0.5 mile you will have climbed to 3,580 feet elevation and reached the junction with Trail 120. Turn left on Trail 120 and head east. The course stays fairly level for the 0.3 mile to the junction with Trail 120b.

Turn left on Trail 120b and begin the descent back toward the trailhead. Soon the route makes a wide switchback to the left and crosses a tiny stream. After the switchback there is a larger stream on the right side of the trail. Soon the track crosses another small stream, which passes beneath the roadbed in a culvert. Bracken fern line the tread as you hike the last part of the route back to the Entrance Loop Trailhead.

Miles and Directions

0.0   Cross the highway from the parking area and hike south-southwest on Trail 120a.

0.5   Turn left at the junction with Trail 120.

0.8   Turn left again at the junction with Trail 120b.

1.5   Return to the Entrance Loop Trailhead.

10 Burping Brook Loop

The Burping Brook Loop traverses a maze of trails, through diverse forests and along bubbling streams. While not very physically demanding, it has enough junctions and turns to be a little challenging. It's a good hike on which to teach children how to follow directions and read maps, while never really getting very far from the trailhead.

Distance: 1.8-mile lollipop loop
Hiking time: About 1 to 1.5 hours
Difficulty: Moderate
Trail surface: Dirt singletrack and gravel roadbed
Best seasons: Summer and early fall
Other trail users: Mountain bikes and horses are also allowed on these trails. Most of this route is marked with blue diamond cross-country ski markers and is a designated ski trail during the winter season.
Canine compatibility: Pets must be on a leash and under physical control at all times.
Fees and permits: Discover Pass, available where fishing licenses are sold or online at www.discover pass.wa.gov. A Snopark permit is required during the winter season.

A grooming sticker may also be needed during winter, depending on where you park.
Schedule: Summer 6:30 a.m. to dusk, winter 6:30 a.m. to 10 p.m.
Maps: Mount Spokane State Park map, produced by Washington State Parks and available at the park entrance booth, or the map in this book
Trail contact: Mount Spokane State Park, 26107 North Mount Spokane Park Dr., Mead, WA 99021; (509) 238-4258; www .parks.wa.gov
Special considerations: The hiking directions below are fairly complicated (more so than the route really is). Keep a close eye on the map in this book as you hike so that you don't miss a turn.

Finding the trailhead: From downtown Spokane head north on Division Street to the junction with US 2 (Newport Highway). Follow US 2 to the junction with SR 206 (Mount Spokane Park Drive). Turn right on SR 206 and drive 17.2 miles to the first junction with the Mount Kit Carson Loop Road and the Lower Loop Road Trailhead. There is a large paved parking area along the road 50 yards southeast of the trailhead but no other facilities. The elevation at the trailhead is 3,880 feet. GPS: N47 54.285' / W117 07.490'

The Hike

Walk north from the parking area along Mount Spokane Park Drive for about 50 yards to the junction with the Mount Kit Carson Loop Road and the trailhead. Take the loop road, heading northwest, and pass the gate, which blocks the road from motor vehicle traffic. In about another 50 yards turn right toward Trail 100, leaving the roadbed. A short distance after leaving the roadbed there will be another trail junction. To the right Trail 100 heads east, and to the left Trail 100 heads west. Bear right and hike northeast for a few yards to another trail junction. Here Trail 100 turns to the right.

Bear left (straight ahead), leaving Trail 100, and climb northeast on the right side of the creek. Shortly the trail, which is a poorly maintained and long-abandoned roadbed, crosses a five-log bridge over a tiny stream. The track climbs, sometimes steeply, through the forest of hemlock, cedar, and fir trees. Below the forest canopy bracken fern, two species of huckleberry bushes, and Rocky Mountain maple make up much of the understory. Before long the trail comes to an end, at 4,130 feet elevation, 0.4 mile from the trailhead. Turn around and retrace your steps back 0.3 mile to the lower junction with Trail 100, at 3,900 feet elevation.

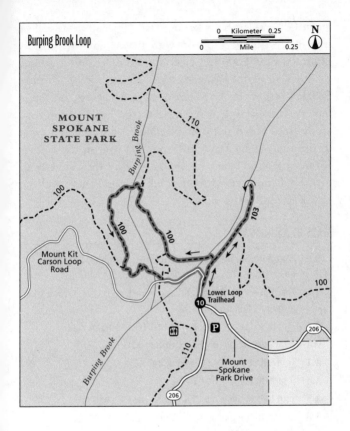

Turn right at the junction and take Trail 100, heading west. Cross the creek and quickly reach the junction with Trail 110. Bear right at the junction and hike northwest. Here Trails 100 and 110 follow the same route. In about 0.3 mile you will come to another trail junction, at 4,040 feet elevation. Bear left here, leaving Trail 110 and staying on Trail 100.

The route quickly crosses Burping Brook then begins to descend. In 0.3 mile you will reach yet another trail junction. Turn left here, leaving Trail 100, and descend five switchbacks to the junction with the Mount Kit Carson Loop Road, at 3,800 feet elevation, 1.5 miles into this hike.

Turn left on the roadbed and head east, crossing Burping Brook as it flows beneath large western red cedars. Just across the creek there is a picnic table to the left, and the road crosses Trail 110. A restroom is located a short distance away, to the right along Trail 110. Continue east on the Mount Kit Carson Loop Road, cross another creek, then head south to the junction with Mount Spokane Park Drive and the Lower Loop Road Trailhead.

Miles and Directions

0.0 Hike north from the Lower Loop Road Trailhead. Pass the junction with Trail 100 on the right and continue.

0.4 The trail ends. Turn around and retrace your route toward the lower junction with Trail 100.

0.7 Return to lower junction with Trail 100 and turn right.

0.8 Bear right at the junction with Trail 110.

1.1 Turn left on Trail 100, leaving Trail 110.

1.4 Bear left, leaving Trail 100.

1.5 Turn left on the Mount Kit Carson Loop Road.

1.8 Return to the junction with Mount Spokane Park Drive and the Lower Loop Road Trailhead.

11 Bald Knob–CCC Cabin

This section of Trail 130 offers an easy hike through forest that is more open than most of the area in Mount Spokane State Park. This openness allows for a wider variety of flowers and low bushes than generally found elsewhere in the park. The CCC (Civilian Conservation Corps) Cabin is usually open and makes a great spot for lunch.

Distance: 2 miles out and back
Hiking time: About 1.5 hours
Difficulty: Easy
Trail surface: Dirt singletrack
Best seasons: Summer and early fall
Other trail users: Mountain bikers, equestrians, and in the winter cross-country skiers
Canine compatibility: Pets must be on a leash and under physical control at all times.
Fees and permits: Discover Pass, available where fishing licenses are sold or online at www.discover pass.wa.gov. A Snopark permit is required during the winter season. A grooming sticker may also be needed during winter, depending on where you park.
Schedule: Summer 6:30 a.m. to dusk, winter 6:30 a.m. to 10 p.m.
Map: Mount Spokane State Park map, produced by Washington State Parks and available at the park entrance booth
Trail contact: Mount Spokane State Park, 26107 North Mount Spokane Park Dr., Mead, WA 99021; (509) 238-4258; www .parks.wa.gov

Finding the trailhead: From downtown Spokane head north on Division Street to the junction with US 2 (Newport Highway). Follow US 2 to the junction with SR 206 (Mount Spokane Park Drive). Turn right on SR 206 and drive 18.5 miles to the junction with the Mount Spokane Summit Road. Turn left on the Mount Spokane Summit Road and go 1.2 miles to the Bald Knob Campground and Trailhead. The trailhead is on the left side of the road, and the campground is on the right. Restrooms and ample parking are available across the road from the trailhead next to the campground. Water is available only during the summer. GPS: N47 54.775' / W117 06.778'

The Hike

Leaving the unmarked trailhead, at 5,120 feet elevation, the route leads northwest through the semi-open subalpine forest. Grand fir, lodgepole pine, and Engelmann spruce make up the mix of conifers, while the ground is covered with beargrass, pearly everlasting, bracken fern, fireweed, and coneflower as well as elderberry and huckleberry bushes. Engelmann spruce, *Picea engelmannii,* is often a microclimate indicator—this is a tree that seems to like cold spots. During cooler times of the year, it's a good idea not to camp in a grove of these sharp-needled trees, unless you want to spend a cold night.

The summit of 5,883-foot-high Mount Spokane looms above to the right as you continue your hike to the west-northwest. In a few places mountain ash bushes crowd the trailside. The red-orange berries of the mountain ash add a spectacular splash of color in late summer.

There will be a trail junction 0.9 mile into the hike. Hike straight ahead (north) at the junction. Then, in a short distance, bear right. In a few more yards the CCC Cabin comes into view above to your right. Turn right and climb the cobblestone steps to the cabin. If it's wet, these steps can be very slick. When you are ready, return as you came to the Bald Knob Trailhead.

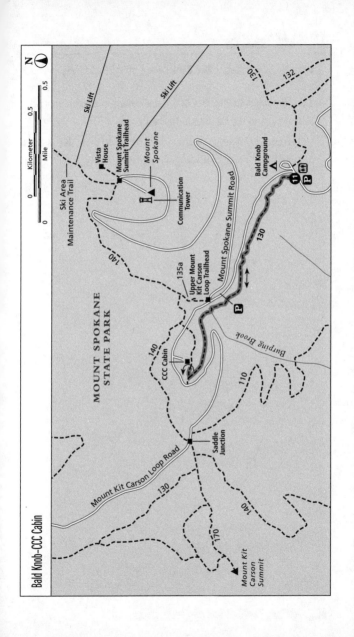

Bald Knob-CCC Cabin

Miles and Directions

0.0   Cross the road to the Bald Knob Trailhead and hike northwest.

1.0   The route reaches the CCC Cabin, your turnaround point.

2.0   Return to the Bald Knob Trailhead.

   Option: Continue to the summit of Mount Kit Carson (Hike 12) and return, adding 3.1 miles to the hike.

12 Mount Kit Carson

Mount Spokane State Park covers 13,643 acres and is Washington's largest state park. In the heart of the park is 5,282-foot-high Mount Kit Carson. While the hike to the summit is only moderately difficult, the view from the top is among the best in the park. Wildlife abounds here, but is often difficult to spot because of the dense vegetation. You will, however, almost undoubtedly see the tracks of deer and elk and possibly those of a moose.

Distance: 3.6 miles out and back
Hiking time: About 2 hours
Difficulty: Moderate, with 0.6 mile that is challenging
Trail surface: Gravel and dirt road, dirt singletrack
Best seasons: Summer and early fall
Other trail users: Mountain bikes and horses are also allowed on most of this route.
Canine compatibility: Pets must be on a leash and under physical control at all times.
Fees and permits: Discover Pass, available where fishing licenses are sold or online at www.discover pass.wa.gov. A Snopark permit is required during the winter season.

A grooming sticker may also be needed during winter, depending on where you park.
Schedule: Summer 6:30 a.m. to dusk, winter 6:30 a.m. to 10 p.m.
Maps: Mount Spokane State Park map, produced by Washington State Parks and available at park entrance booth. Older maps may show Trail 140 as Trail 115 and/or Trail 135. The National Geographic Washington topo on CD-ROM Disk 4 shows most of the route.
Trail contact: Mount Spokane State Park, 26107 North Mount Spokane Park Dr., Mead, WA 99021; (509) 238-4258; www .parks.wa.gov

Finding the trailhead: From downtown Spokane head north on Division Street to the junction with US 2 (Newport Highway). Follow

US 2 to the junction with SR 206 (Mount Spokane Park Drive). Turn right on SR 206 and drive 18.5 miles to the junction with the Mount Spokane Summit Road. Turn left on the Mount Spokane Summit Road and go 1.8 miles to the junction with the Mount Kit Carson Loop Road, which is the Upper Mount Kit Carson Loop Trailhead. There is adequate parking in the lot on the right side of the road, approximately 60 yards southeast of the trailhead, but no other facilities. The elevation at the trailhead is 5,200 feet. GPS: N45 55.067'/W117 07.377'

The Hike

Walk northwest from the parking area, up the Mount Spokane Summit Road for about 60 yards to the junction with the Mount Kit Carson Loop Road, which is the starting point of this hike. Step around the white metal gate and hike northwest along the Loop Road, through the forest of mountain ash, alder, and fir trees. In slightly more than 0.1 mile you will reach a junction. There is a sign here directing bikes to stay on the Loop Road. Turn left on the abandoned roadbed and follow it west, over the top of Beauty Mountain, to the CCC (Civilian Conservation Corps) Cabin. The route is closed to all but hikers from the Loop Road to the CCC Cabin.

At the CCC Cabin you are 0.25 mile from the trailhead. As you approach the cabin, ignore the roadbed to the right. Walk around the left (south) side of the cabin to its front door, which is on the west side. The cabin is generally unlocked and open to the public. (*Option:* This hike may be combined with the Bald Knob–CCC Cabin hike [Hike 11] when you return to this point, if you have a car shuttle available to the Bald Knob Campground and Trailhead.)

To continue the hike to the summit of Mount Kit Carson, descend the cobblestone steps and follow the route to the west. In a short distance there will be an unmarked trail junction; turn left (south). A short distance farther is another trail junction; turn right here and descend the last few feet to rejoin the Mount Kit Carson Loop Road. Turn left on the road. In 0.2 mile the roadbed makes a switchback to the right, then continues to descend gently west-northwest to Saddle Junction. There are restrooms available at Saddle Junction (elevation 4,890 feet). The Mount Spokane Summit–Saddle Junction hike (Hike 13) also reaches this saddle.

Several trails meet at the junction; the one toward the summit of Mount Kit Carson is Trail 170. Trail signs point the way here. The course climbs west-southwest, leaving Saddle Junction. In a bit less than 0.2 mile you will reach the junction with Trail 140. Bear slightly right here and continue to climb the now quite steep route. Huckleberry bushes line this part of the trail beneath the high mountain forest canopy. About 20 yards past the junction with Trail 140 there will be another path to the right. Stay on the main trail and keep on climbing to the southwest. The track gets narrower as you ascend.

The route flattens out on the summit ridge of Mount Kit Carson, 0.3 mile from the junction with Trail 140. In another 0.1 mile there will be yet another trail junction. Bear left (nearly straight ahead) here and leave Trail 170. The last 0.1 mile to the summit is on an unnumbered trail, but it appears to be the main trail here. Scramble up the last few feet to the summit of Mount Kit Carson.

The rocky summit, at 5,282 feet, has great views in all directions. Close by to the east-northeast is Mount Spokane, and to the southwest, often through the haze, is the city of Spokane. The summit is the turnaround point of this hike, so retrace your steps back to the trailhead.

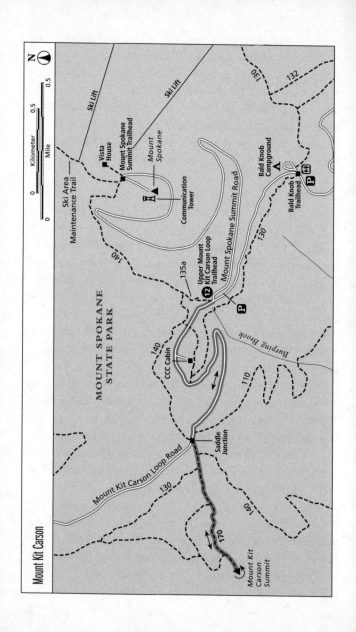

Mount Kit Carson

Miles and Directions

0.0 Hike northwest from the Upper Mount Kit Carson Loop Trailhead.

0.1 Turn left on an abandoned roadbed, leaving the Mount Kit Carson Loop Road.

0.3 The route reaches the CCC Cabin.

1.1 Turn left onto Trail 170 at Saddle Junction.

1.3 Bear slightly to the right and continue to climb steeply past Trail 140.

1.7 Bear slightly left (nearly straight ahead) at the trail junction, heading southwest, leaving Trail 170.

1.8 The route reaches the summit of Mount Kit Carson, your turnaround point.

3.6 Return to the Upper Mount Kit Carson Loop Trailhead.

13 Mount Spokane Summit-Saddle Junction

This lollipop loop descends from the subalpine summit of Mount Spokane then climbs back up, making it an excellent conditioning hike. There is one very short section (about 100 yards long) of trail that was difficult to see on the ground when I last hiked this route. The rest of the route is on obvious trails and a roadbed.

Distance: 3.5-mile lollipop loop
Hiking time: About 2.5 hours
Difficulty: Challenging, with a very short section that requires some route-finding skills
Trail surface: Dirt singletrack and dirt road
Best seasons: Summer and early fall
Other trail users: Equestrians and mountain bikers
Canine compatibility: Pets must be on a leash and under physical control at all times.
Fees and Permits: Discover Pass, available where fishing licenses are sold or online at www.discover pass.wa.gov.

Schedule: Summer 6:30 a.m. to dusk, winter 6:30 a.m. to 10 p.m.
Map: Mount Spokane State Park map, produced by Washington State Parks and available at park entrance booth. Older maps may show Trail 140 as Trail 135.
Trail contact: Mount Spokane State Park, 26107 North Mount Spokane Park Dr., Mead, WA 99021; (509) 238-4258; www .parks.wa.gov
Special considerations: Use caution when following the Trail 135a portion of this route. It is not maintained and is vague, but it is very short.

Finding the trailhead: From downtown Spokane head north on Division Street to the junction with US 2 (Newport Highway). Follow

US 2 to the junction with SR 206 (Mount Spokane Park Drive). Turn right on SR 206 and drive 18.5 miles to the junction with the Mount Spokane Summit Road. Turn left on the Mount Spokane Summit Road and go 4 miles to the summit of Mount Spokane and the trailhead. The trailhead is on the right just past the trail to Vista House. There is parking for several vehicles at the trailhead but no other facilities. GPS: N47 55.360' / W117 06.812'

The Hike

Hike northwest, leaving the 5,870-foot-high trailhead near the summit of Mount Spokane. The rough and rocky route descends steeply through the short subalpine timber and beargrass. After descending about 200 vertical feet, the track makes a couple of switchbacks. You cross a sloping meadow 0.4 mile into the hike and soon pass Mile Marker 5. When you reach the mile marker, you will have descended to 5,450 feet elevation. In the semi-open woods bracken fern, pearly everlasting, and fireweed cover the ground, with huckleberry and elderberry bushes growing above the flowers.

There will be a very vague path to the left 0.9 mile from the trailhead. This path is Trail 135a, which is part of your return route; don't take it now. This is where the loop portion of the hike begins. There is a much more obvious path to the left 0.1 mile farther along, which leads to the Mount Kit Carson Loop Road. Bear right and head west, staying on Trail 140. The course descends a little more, then traverses the wooded slope to Saddle Junction, passing Mile Marker 4 shortly before reaching it. Saddle Junction, at 4,890 feet elevation and 1.6 miles from the trailhead, is the junction of Trails 140, 110, and 170 and the Mount Kit Carson Loop Road, which is closed to unauthorized motor vehicles. There is a restroom at Saddle Junction.

To continue your hike, turn left on the Mount Kit Carson Loop Road and walk southeast. In 0.4 mile the route makes a switchback to head northwest. A little over 0.1 mile farther you reach the junction with Trail 130, which is to the right. Don't take the trail; stay on the loop road. In 0.1 mile there will be a wooden gate and a junction with a spur road, which leads to the CCC (Civilian Conservation Corps) Cabin. The cabin is but a short distance up this spur road if you would like to visit it. To continue, hike straight ahead on the main road.

The road passes two more trail junctions in the next 0.25 mile before reaching the junction with the Mount Spokane Summit Road and Trail 135a. The trail to the right leads back to the CCC Cabin. The one to the left goes a few yards to Trail 140 (the one you descended to Saddle Junction on). Continue along the Loop Road to the junction with the Mount Spokane Summit Road, at 5,200 feet elevation.

At the junction there will be another dirt road to the left (north). Take this road, which is Trail 135a, and hike northerly for a bit less than 0.1 mile to a radio tower. This is where the route becomes very vague. Walk between the tower and the building next to it. Continue generally north, crossing a tiny stream. In about 100 yards you will intersect Trail 140. The tower should be in view through the trees all the way to Trail 140. Trail 135a is there, but it is hard to spot on the ground. This unsigned junction is the end the loop part of this hike. Turn right on Trail 140 and retrace your steps, climbing back to the trailhead near the summit of Mount Spokane.

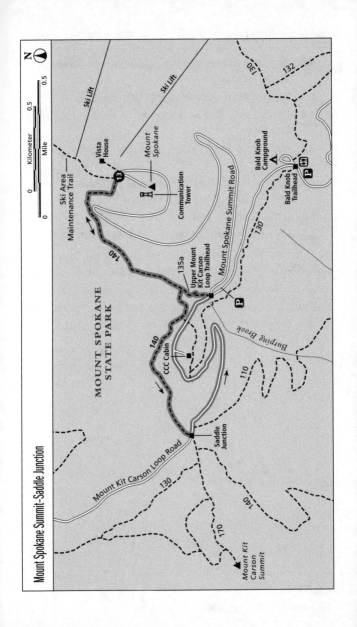

Mount Spokane Summit–Saddle Junction

Miles and Directions

0.0 Begin your descent from the trailhead near the summit of Mount Spokane.

0.9 Pass the slightly obscure junction with Trail 135a.

1.6 Reach Saddle Junction and turn left on the Mount Kit Carson Loop Road.

2.2 Hike straight ahead at the junction with roadbed to the CCC Cabin.

2.5 Reach the junction with the Mount Spokane Summit Road and Trail 135a. Turn left on Trail 135a.

2.6 Turn right on Trail 140.

3.5 Return to the trailhead near the summit of Mount Spokane.

Option: For a longer hike, continue west from Saddle Junction to the summit of Mount Kit Carson and return before climbing back to the trailhead at the summit of Mount Spokane. The Mount Kit Carson hike description (Hike 12) covers this route. This side trip will add 1.4 challenging miles to your hike.

14 Liberty Creek Loop

The Liberty Creek Loop is one of the most rewarding hikes covered in this book. It is, however, also one of the most difficult. The route takes you from the marshland at the south end of Liberty Lake through mixed forests that consist of three species of pines as well as grand and Douglas fir, western hemlock, western red cedar, and several deciduous species. You climb more than 1,200 feet to reach Camp Hughes before descending back to lake level.

Distance: 7.4-mile lollipop loop
Hiking time: About 3.5 to 5 hours
Difficulty: Challenging
Trail surface: Gravel at the start, then smooth dirt, along an abandoned roadbed to Liberty Creek Cedar Forest. The next 1.6-mile section to Camp Hughes is a rough and eroded dirt singletrack. The return section from Camp Hughes back to the trailhead is mostly along an abandoned dirt roadbed.
Best seasons: Summer and fall
Other trail users: Bikes are often ridden along this route. Stock is permitted on most of the return portion (west side) of this loop.
Canine compatibility: Leashed dogs are permitted.
Fees and permits: None

Schedule: The trail is open year-round, 24/7, and camping is permitted along it in places. However, the trailhead, campground, and road leading to the campground are closed during the winter months.
Maps: Liberty Lake and Mica Peak USGS 7.5-minute quads cover the area. The National Geographic Washington topo on CD-ROM Disk 4 covers the area and shows parts of the route. Check out the map on the reader board at the trailhead before you start hiking, and use the one in this book.
Trail contact: Spokane County Parks and Recreation, 404 North Havana St., Spokane, WA 99202; (509) 477-4730

Special considerations: The Liberty Creek Loop is moderately long, as easy day hikes go, and has a 1.6-mile section that is not very easy, being steep and narrow in places. However, the rest of the route generally follows abandoned roadbeds and is easy.

Finding the trailhead: From I-90 at exit 296, drive south 0.2 mile to Appleway Avenue. Turn left (east) on Appleway and go 0.9 mile to Molter Road. Turn right (south) on Molter Road, following the small signs toward Liberty Lake County Park, and drive 1.1 miles to Valley Way. Turn left on Valley Way and head east for 0.8 mile. The road then turns right (south) and becomes Lakeside Road. Follow Lakeside Road for 1.6 miles to Zepher Road. Turn right on Zepher Road and soon enter Liberty Lake County Park. You will reach the campground and trailhead 0.8 mile after turning on Zepher Road. The trailhead is at the southwest corner of the campground. There is parking for several cars at the trailhead. A fee is charged for camping. The elevation at the trailhead is 2,060 feet. GPS: N47 37.855'/W117 03.512'

If you plan to use the lower portion of this trail during the winter or early spring (the higher country will probably be snowed in), the road from the park entrance booth to the campground may be closed. In this case, turn right at the entrance booth and drive a short distance to the parking area next to the playground equipment. From this parking area, walk south along the east side of the marshland on a path, passing a boardwalk that leads to a viewing platform. The path soon joins a service road, which leads to the campground and trailhead. The added distance is only about 0.2 mile.

The Hike

This loop hike begins and ends on the Liberty Creek Trail, which leaves from the south end of Liberty Lake County Park Campground. Stop and read the reader board, then pass through a gate and begin your hike on the broad gravel trail.

There will be a path to the left slightly over 0.1 mile from the trailhead. Stay on the main trail (straight ahead), heading south-southeast. The gravel ends here and the trail surface becomes dirt.

The loop begins at the junction with the Edith Hanson Cut-Off Trail, 0.3 mile from the trailhead. The loop can be hiked in either direction but this description is clockwise, so bear left (straight ahead to the south). Horses are not allowed on this side of the loop but bikes are. Continue south-southeast through the mixed forest, climbing very gently. A little over 1 mile from the trailhead the trail splits. Take the left fork and cross a wooden bridge over Split Creek. After crossing the creek the trails quickly rejoin. You will cross a couple more small wooden bridges and traverse a couple sections of boardwalk over wet areas in the mile from the Split Creek crossing to the Liberty Creek Cedar Forest. At 2,500 feet elevation, this is the end of the gentle broad trail for a while. Take the time to read the informational signs here.

Bear to the right at the Cedar Forest, cross a creek on a wooden bridge, and begin the steepest part of this hike. The now narrow and steep route makes eleven switchbacks in the next 0.3 mile, as you climb to a viewpoint at 2,790 feet elevation. The view is to the north, overlooking Liberty Lake.

Past the viewpoint the track crosses a couple tiny streams, which may be dry, then makes a couple more switchbacks before crossing a wooden bridge just below a small waterfall. By the time you reach the bridge and waterfall, you will have climbed to 2,870 feet elevation and are 3.1 miles from the trailhead. Above the waterfall the tread continues to climb, making fourteen more switchbacks in the next 0.5 mile. The course then crosses the creek on a wooden bridge.

The trail soon leaves the creek behind and continues to climb. You will cross an abandoned roadbed, with a sign next to it that says MORE HIKING. Hike straight ahead, climbing a short distance to the top of a rise, at 3,260 feet elevation.

The tread then passes a short side trail that leads to an outhouse, before descending the last few yards to Camp Hughes. Camp Hughes consists of a small cabin with a fireplace and bunks, as well as an outside fire pit. The bunks are in poor condition at the present time. At Camp Hughes you are 3.7 miles into the hike at 3,250 feet elevation.

The Edith Hanson Riding Trail, which you will be following for the next 3.2 miles, turns left next to the cabin. The course descends a short distance to a junction with an abandoned roadbed, which will serve as the trail much of the way back to the trailhead. This section of the trail is open to stock. Turn left on the roadbed and start a very gentle descent. The broad tread crosses a tiny stream in 0.4 mile, then begins to descend a bit more steeply in places. A mile farther along, the track crosses another small stream. Two miles from Camp Hughes, at 2,860 feet elevation, another trail (abandoned roadbed) joins the one you are hiking on. Hike straight ahead, continuing to descend. There are no signs at this junction.

A SCENIC OVERLOOK sign is reached 0.1 mile after passing the unmarked junction; unfortunately, trees obstruct much of the view. A couple tenths of a mile farther is another unmarked trail junction. Bear slightly right here, staying on the main trail, and descend a few yards to the junction with the Scenic Trail. This signed junction, at 2,690 feet elevation, is 6 miles from the trailhead where you started.

Continue straight ahead and descend moderately. A couple tenths of a mile farther along, Liberty Lake comes

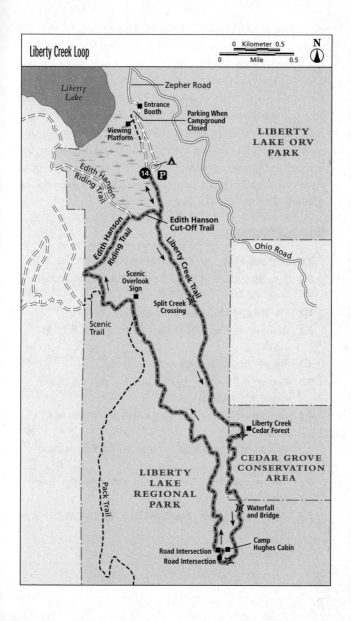

Liberty Creek Loop

0   Kilometer   0.5

0   Mile   0.5

N

Liberty Lake

Zepher Road

Entrance Booth

Parking When Campground Closed

LIBERTY LAKE ORV PARK

Viewing Platform

Edith Hanson Riding Trail

14   P

Edith Hanson Cut-Off Trail

Edith Hanson Riding Trail

Ohio Road

Liberty Creek Trail

Scenic Overlook Sign

Split Creek Crossing

Scenic Trail

Liberty Creek Cedar Forest

CEDAR GROVE CONSERVATION AREA

LIBERTY LAKE REGIONAL PARK

Waterfall and Bridge

Pack Trail

Camp Hughes Cabin

Road Intersection

Road Intersection

into view ahead, through the trees. In another 0.5 mile the route passes through a gate and flattens out. Shortly you will reach the junction with the Edith Hanson Cut-Off Trail. Close to the junction a sign commemorates Edith Hanson, for whom these trails were named. Hike straight ahead here, heading northeast on the Edith Hanson Cut-Off Trail (the Edith Hanson Riding Trail turns to the left). Soon the tread turns to the east, crosses a couple of sluggish streams, and reaches the junction with the Liberty Creek Trail to complete the loop. Turn left here and retrace your steps the last 0.3 mile back to the trailhead.

Miles and Directions

0.0 Hike south from the Liberty Lake County Park and Trailhead.

0.3 Bear left (straight ahead to the south) at the trail junction to begin the loop.

1.1 The trail reaches Split Creek crossing.

2.1 At the Liberty Creek Cedar Forest, turn right and begin to climb.

3.1 The trail crosses a bridge below a waterfall.

3.7 Turn left at the Camp Hughes Cabin and descend to an abandoned roadbed.

6.0 Bear right, staying on the main trail at the junction with the Scenic Trail.

6.9 Hike straight ahead at the junction with the Edith Hanson Cut-Off Trail.

7.1 Junction with Liberty Creek Trail and end of the loop. Turn left.

7.4 Return to the Liberty Lake County Park and Trailhead.

15 Blackwell Island Wetland Trail

The Blackwell Island Wetland Trail is a short stroll through an interesting wetland area next to the Spokane River, a short distance south of Coeur d'Alene, Idaho. The area gets its name from the Blackwell Lumber Company, which had a mill close to here from 1909 to 1937. This mill was for a time one of the largest lumber producers in the region.

Distance: 0.3-mile loop
Hiking time: About 20 minutes
Difficulty: Very easy, barrier free
Trail surface: Concrete sidewalk and wide boardwalk trail
Best seasons: Spring, summer, and fall. The official season is Memorial Day through mid-Oct.
Other trail users: Hikers only. This trail is wheelchair accessible.
Canine compatibility: Dogs must be kept on a leash.

Fees and permits: Parking fee
Schedule: 5 a.m. to 11 p.m. Memorial Day through mid-Oct
Maps: The map on the reader board or the one in this book is more than adequate.
Trail contact: US Department of the Interior, Bureau of Land Management, Coeur d'Alene Field Office, 3815 Schreiber Way, Coeur d'Alene, ID 83815; (208) 769-5000

Finding the trailhead: Take exit 12 off I-90 at Coeur d'Alene. From the exit take US 95 south for 1.4 miles, crossing the bridge over the Spokane River. The Blackwell Island Recreation Area and the trailhead are on the right side of the highway. The trail begins at the northeast corner of the easternmost parking area. There is plenty of parking and restrooms at the trailhead. The elevation at the trailhead is approximately 2,130 feet. GPS: N47 41.118'/W116 48.279'

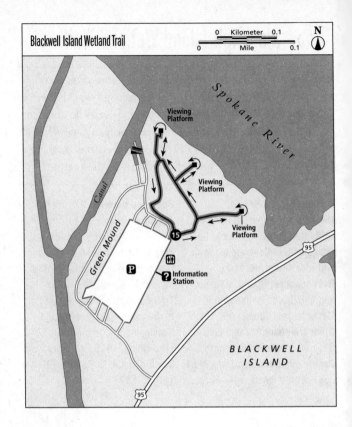

Blackwell Island Wetland Trail

Viewing Platform

Viewing Platform

Viewing Platform

15

Spokane River

Canal

Green Mound

P

Information Station

95

95

BLACKWELL ISLAND

N

Kilometer

Mile

The Hike

The boardwalk route heads northeast from the parking area. In a few yards you will come to a junction; turn right and walk northeasterly, through a grove of tall cottonwood trees. You will reach the first viewing platform in about 100 yards. Benches on the platform make this a great place to sit a while and watch the waterfowl and other wetland wildlife close to the Spokane River.

When you're ready, walk back to the junction, turn right, and walk about 50 yards to the next junction. Turn right and follow the boardwalk across the marshland to the second viewing platform, also close to the Spokane River. Return to the main trail and turn right (westerly) again.

Shortly you will reach yet another trail junction; turn right and walk to the third and final viewing platform. Then return to the main trail, bear right (straight ahead), and hike the short distance, through the lodgepole and ponderosa pines and black hawthorn bushes, to the end of the boardwalk. Black hawthorn, *Crataegus douglasii,* also called native hawthorn and thorn brush, is a short stocky tree or large bush. The huge thorns, sometimes up to 1.5 inches long, were often used by native people and pioneers as needles and fishhooks. They can cause painful punctures and cuts if you try to force your way through the brush.

From the end of the boardwalk, follow the sidewalk southeast back to the trailhead, ending the loop hike.

Miles and Directions

0.0   Walk northeast from the trailhead.

0.2   Turn right and walk to the last viewing platform, then return to the main trail.

0.3   Return to the trailhead.

16 English Point Yellow Loop

The English Point Yellow Loop (Trail 80) is the longest of the five loop trails in the English Point Trail System. Somewhat unusual in this suburban setting, these trails are on an isolated parcel of national forest land. Because of the gentle grade of the route and the possibility of taking one of the shorter loops if some in the party are getting tired, this makes a great hike for families with kids. This trail is designated a National Recreation Trail.

Distance: 3.2-mile lollipop loop
Hiking time: About 1.5 hours
Difficulty: Easy to moderate
Trail surface: Wide dirt singletrack
Best seasons: Spring, summer, and fall, or cross-country skiing in the winter
Other trail users: Hikers, equestrians, mountain bikers, and cross-country skiers
Canine compatibility: Dogs are permitted but must be kept under control.
Fees and permits: None
Schedule: 24/7

Maps: The map on the reader board at the trailhead or the map in this book should be all that is needed. The USGS Hayden Lake quad covers the area. The National Geographic Idaho topo on CD-ROM covers the area but shows these trails somewhat inaccurately.
Trail contact: USDA Forest Service, Coeur d'Alene River Ranger District, Fernan Office, 2502 East Sherman Ave., Coeur d'Alene, ID 83814; (208) 664-2318

Finding the trailhead: Take exit 12 off I-90 at Coeur d'Alene. From the exit drive north on US 95 for 6 miles to the junction with Lancaster Road. Turn right on Lancaster and go 3.5 miles east to the junction with English Point Road. Turn right on English Point Road and quickly turn left into the parking area at the English Point Trail-head. Plenty of parking and restrooms are available at the trailhead. The Yellow Loop begins on the opposite (west) side of English Point Road from the parking area, at an elevation of 2,580 feet. GPS: N47 47.256' / W116 42.694'

The Hike

Cross English Point Road, angling slightly north to find the trailhead for the Yellow, Blue, and Green Trails. Stop and check out the maps and signs at the trailhead, then begin your hike, heading southwest. All three of the loop trails (Yellow, Green, and Blue) follow the same route for the first 0.5 mile. The loops are marked with cross-country diamonds on the trees beside the trail. The color of the diamond corresponds to the name of the trail. (Follow the yellow diamonds to stay on the Yellow Loop.) In 0.1 mile there will be a trail junction; bear left. The track heads southeast for a short distance then turns south, close to English Point Road. The course soon turns south-west again and reaches a trail junction 0.5 mile from the trailhead.

At this junction the Blue Loop turns to the right. Bear left, staying on the Yellow and Green Loops and continu-ing to walk beneath the Douglas firs and ponderosa pines. Beside the tread rose bushes add a splash of color both with their blooms and their bright orange hips. A little less than 0.5 mile after leaving the junction with the Blue Loop, there will be a poor trail to the left; don't take it. Soon you will reach a trail junction with benches next to it. This junction, 1 mile from the trailhead, is where the Green Loop leaves the Yellow Loop. Bear left on the boardwalk and pass a small pond to continue on the Yellow Loop. Now only yellow diamonds mark the route. Several poor paths leave the trail, but it is easy to follow the Yellow Loop.

The route approaches a paved road 0.5 mile farther along. To the left through the trees is a view of Hayden Lake. The course crosses a short wooden boardwalk 2.1 miles into the hike. In another 0.2 mile the trail forks, with yellow diamonds going both ways. Bear left and descend. The forks quickly rejoin each other. The trail to the right is an easier way for cross-country skiers to descend and ascend this short but steep hill. The track soon crosses a wooden bridge, then climbs a short distance. Shortly there will be a field to the left and a view of mountains and houses. The course passes a large house and soon crosses another bridge. One-tenth mile after crossing the bridge, the route rejoins the Green Loop. This junction is 2.9 miles into the hike. Turn left and hike north on the now combined Yellow and Green Loops.

A little less than 0.2 mile more brings you to the junction with the Blue Loop. Bear left (nearly straight ahead) and continue hiking northeast, passing the junction where all the loops begin, back to the trailhead.

Miles and Directions

0.0 Cross English Point Road, then hike southwest from the trailhead.

0.1 Turn left at the trail junction to start the loop portion of this hike.

0.5 Bear left, passing the junction with the Blue Trail.

1.0 Bear left on the boardwalk as you pass a trail junction and a bench.

2.3 The trail forks; bear left and descend a short distance.

2.9 Turn left at the junction with the Green Trail.

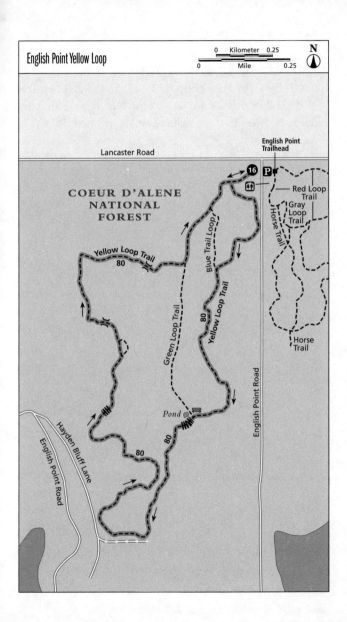

English Point Yellow Loop

0   Kilometer   0.25

0   Mile   0.25

N

Lancaster Road

English Point
Trailhead

16   P

COEUR D'ALENE
NATIONAL
FOREST

Red Loop
Trail

Gray
Loop
Trail

Blue Trail Loop

Horse Trail

Yellow Loop Trail

80

Green Loop Trail

Yellow Loop Trail

80

English Point Road

Horse
Trail

Pond

80

Hayden Bluff Lane

English Point Road

80

3.1 Bear left (nearly straight ahead) at the junction with the Blue Trail.

3.2 Return to the English Point Trailhead.

Options: The Red Loop (Hike 17) and Gray Loop Trails on the other side of English Point Road make excellent additional hikes to enjoy while you are at English Point.

17 English Point Red Loop

The Red Loop Trail is a very pleasant hike through widely diverse second-growth forest, with a couple of viewpoints thrown in for good measure. This is a good hike for all but the smallest children (unless they are in a kiddy pack).

Distance: 1.6-mile loop
Hiking time: About 1 hour
Difficulty: Easy
Trail surface: Gravel singletrack
Best seasons: Spring, summer, and fall
Other trail users: Hikers only; however, horse trails cross the route.
Canine compatibility: Dogs are permitted but must be kept under control.
Fees and permits: None
Schedule: 24/7

Maps: The map on the reader board at the trailhead or the map in this book should be all that is needed. The USGS Hayden Lake quad covers the area. The National Geographic Idaho topo on CD-ROM covers the area but shows these trails somewhat inaccurately.
Trail contact: USDA Forest Service, Coeur d'Alene River Ranger District, Fernan Office, 2502 East Sherman Ave., Coeur d'Alene, ID 83814; (208) 664-2318

Finding the trailhead: Take exit 12 off I-90 at Coeur d'Alene. From the exit drive north on US 95 for 6 miles to the junction with Lancaster Road. Turn right on Lancaster and go 3.5 miles east to the junction with English Point Road. Turn right on English Point Road and quickly turn left into the parking area at the English Point Trailhead. Plenty of parking and restrooms are available at the trailhead. GPS: N47 47.250' / W116 42.619'

The Hike

The Gray Loop Trail and the Red Loop Trail follow the same route for the first 0.4 and the last 0.3 mile of this hike. Walk east from the parking area, through the gate. After passing the gate, quickly bear left. The route descends very gently through the Douglas fir and ponderosa pine woods. The trail is in great condition, with rubber water bars every few yards to prevent erosion.

A path to the left 0.25 mile into the hike leads a few feet to a bench. Bear right, staying on the main trail. The track climbs slightly and soon reaches the first junction with the Gray Loop. Bear left, unless you want to shorten your hike by 0.8 mile by taking the Gray Loop.

Leaving the junction with the Gray Loop, the Red Loop heads south through the forest, which now includes grand fir, aspen, lodgepole pine, and western larch. Western larch, *Larix occidentalis,* is a different kind of conifer—it is deciduous (sheds its leaves). The larch, often called tamarack, turns bright yellow in the fall then sheds its needles, making it look like a dead tree. Tamarack is the wood that most locals prefer to burn in their wood stoves.

To the left of the course, 0.3 mile after leaving the junction with the Gray Loop, is a viewpoint with benches. A few yards farther along, 0.9 mile from the trailhead, is another viewpoint, this one with a wooden platform and benches. The view extends to Hayden Lake and beyond. To the right is a horse and bike trail, which has a dirt surface; there is also a hitching post here. Bear left (nearly straight ahead) to stay on the Red Loop.

Slightly over 0.1 mile past the platform, the route crosses the horse trail and goes through a gate that prevents horse

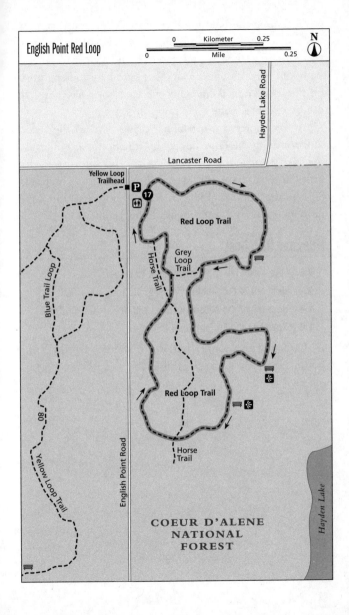

English Point Red Loop

0 Kilometer 0.25
0 Mile 0.25

N

Hayden Lake Road

Lancaster Road

Yellow Loop Trailhead

P
17

Red Loop Trail

Grey Loop Trail

Horse Trail

Blue Trail Loop

80

Yellow Loop Trail

English Point Road

Red Loop Trail

Horse Trail

COEUR D'ALENE NATIONAL FOREST

Hayden Lake

passage along the Red Loop. A short distance farther along, the trail becomes a boardwalk for a few yards. The track passes another bench and soon reaches another junction with a horse trail. There is another gate here to keep horses off the Red Loop. Remember the Red Loop has gravel; the others, except for the Gray Loop, don't.

A few more yards of hiking brings you to the second junction with the Gray Loop. This junction is 1.3 miles into the hike. Bear left at the junction and hike northwest. In a little more than 0.1 mile you will cross a horse trail again. Shortly the horse trail joins the Red Loop, and in 0.1 mile more you return to the English Point Trailhead.

Miles and Directions

0.0 Hike east from the English Point Trailhead.
0.4 Bear left at the first junction with the Gray Loop Trail.
1.3 Bear left at the second junction with the Gray Loop Trail.
1.6 Return to the English Point Trailhead.

Option: For a longer but also easy hike, try the Yellow Loop (Hike 16) across English Point Road from the parking area.

18 Mineral Ridge National Recreation Trail

Besides being an excellent hike with great views, the Mineral Ridge Trail is both a history and natural history lesson. In the direction described below, the upgrades are very moderate. Benches along the way make pleasant rest stops, if you are so inclined.

Distance: 2.8-mile lollipop loop

Hiking time: About 1.5 to 2 hours

Difficulty: Moderate

Trail surface: Dirt singletrack

Best seasons: Late spring, summer, and early fall

Other trail users: Hikers only

Canine compatibility: Leashed dogs are permitted.

Fees and permits: None

Schedule: 24/7

Maps: The map in the BLM *Mineral Ridge Trail Guide,* available at the trailhead, or the one in this book is more than adequate for this hike. The Coeur d'Alene Mountain USGS quad also covers the area. The National Geographic Idaho topo on CD-ROM covers the area and shows this trail as a roadbed.

Trail contact: US Department of the Interior, Bureau of Land Management, Coeur d'Alene Field Office, 3815 Schreiber Way, Coeur d'Alene, ID 83815; (208) 769-5000

Special considerations: If possible, don't leave valuables in your car at this trailhead. If you must leave them, at least hide them or lock them in your trunk, and be sure to lock your car.

Other: Pick up a BLM *Mineral Ridge Trail Guide* if available at the trailhead. This history and natural history guide to the Mineral Ridge Trail is very interesting and is a great help in identifying and understanding the flora, fauna, and mining history of the area. Numbered spots along the trail correspond to numbers in the guide.

Finding the trailhead: Ten miles east of Coeur d'Alene, take exit 22 off I-90. Then head south and west for 2.2 miles on SH 97. The trailhead will be on the left side of SH 97. There are restrooms and parking for about fifteen cars at the trailhead. The elevation at the trailhead is 2,150 feet. GPS: N47 36.920' / W116 40.713'

The Hike

Climb the barrier-free walk from the parking area to the reader board. Take the time to read about the area, and pick up a *Mineral Ridge Trail Guide* booklet. Past the reader board, climb the steps and get on the trail, which climbs gently to the west. Soon the route makes the first of three climbing switchbacks. You then reach a trail junction where the loop portion of this hike begins. Bear right (nearly straight ahead) and hike east, beneath the canopy of Douglas fir and ponderosa pine trees. The track makes a couple more switchbacks as you continue to climb.

The course crosses an abandoned roadbed 0.2 mile after starting the loop. A quarter mile farther along, a sign beside the trail states RADIO ELEVATION 2,705. The sign, which is at approximately 2,470 feet elevation, refers to the Radio Mining Company, which had some underground tunnels in the area, rather than having anything to do with radios.

The trail reaches the junction with the spur trail that goes to an abandoned prospect 0.2 mile after passing the Radio sign. This junction, at 2,550 feet elevation, is 0.9 mile from the trailhead. A sign here states that it is 400 feet to the abandoned prospect along the trail to the left. It is, however, slightly farther than that.

Turn left at the junction and follow the trail to the prospect hole. After inspecting the diggings, and maybe sitting on the bench beside them and taking in the view, return to the main trail. Turn left on the main trail to continue on your Mineral Ridge hike.

A little more than 0.4 mile farther along, the main trail brings you to the 2,780-foot-high ridgeline, a water fountain, and the junction with the Wilson Trail. To the right the Wilson Trail and its extension, the Lost Man Trail (Hike 19), climb to the east and south for 0.8 mile to join Elk Mountain Road (FR 1575). Turn left at the junction and walk a short distance west to the Caribou Cabin. Check out the cabin and the view to the north, then hike west along the ridgeline.

In a little more than 0.3 mile the track reaches the Gray Wolf Viewpoint, with its view of Coeur d'Alene Lake and the I-90 freeway. Another 0.25 mile west along the ridge brings you to the Silver Tip Viewpoint and an even better view of Coeur d'Alene Lake. Past the Silver Tip Viewpoint the trail begins to descend fairly steeply, leaving the ridgeline of Mineral Ridge. The course makes eleven switchbacks in the 0.8 mile to the trail junction at the end of the loop, losing a bit over 500 feet of elevation along the way. Turn right at the junction and retrace your steps for 0.2 mile to the trailhead.

Miles and Directions

0.0 Leaving the Mineral Ridge Trailhead, climb the steps then continue to climb the trail, heading west.

0.2 Bear right at a trail junction and begin the loop.

0.9 Turn left at a junction and head for an abandoned prospect hole.

1.0 Turn around after inspecting the abandoned prospect hole.

1.1 Return to main trail and turn left.

Mineral Ridge National Recreation Trail

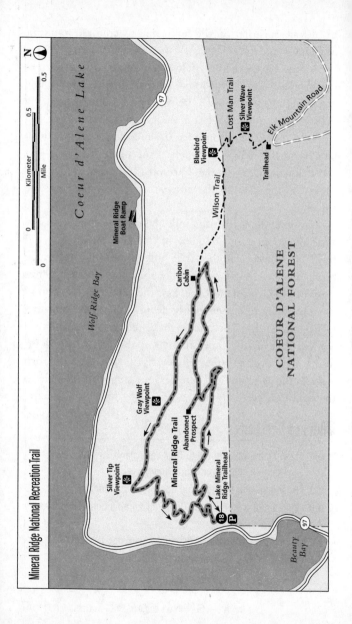

N

Coeur d'Alene Lake

Wolf Ridge Bay

Beauty Bay

Mineral Ridge Boat Ramp

Silver Tip Viewpoint

Gray Wolf Viewpoint

Mineral Ridge Trail

Abandoned Prospect

Lake Mineral Ridge Trailhead

Caribou Cabin

Wilson Trail

Bluebird Viewpoint

Lost Man Trail

Silver Wave Viewpoint

Trailhead

Elk Mountain Road

COEUR D'ALENE NATIONAL FOREST

97

18

P

Kilometer   0.5
Mile   0.5
0

1.5 Turn left at the junction with the Wilson Trail near Caribou Cabin.

1.8 Pass the Gray Wolf Viewpoint.

2.6 Reach the trail junction, ending the loop, and turn right.

2.8 Return to the Mineral Ridge Trailhead.

19 Lost Man Trail

The Lost Man Trail and its continuation, the Wilson Trail, connect the Mineral Ridge National Recreation Trail with an obscure trailhead on Elk Mountain Road atop Mineral Ridge. These trails can also be easily hiked, in the opposite direction from what is described below, as a side trip when hiking the Mineral Ridge Trail. However you decide to hike these short trails, the views are well worth the effort.

Distance: 1.6 miles out and back
Hiking time: About 1 hour
Difficulty: Moderate
Trail surface: Dirt singletrack
Best seasons: Late spring, summer, and early fall
Other trail users: Hikers only
Canine compatibility: Leashed dogs are permitted.
Fees and permits: None
Schedule: 24/7

Maps: The map in the BLM *Mineral Ridge Trail Guide,* generally available at the Mineral Ridge Trailhead, or the one in this book are more than adequate for this hike. The Coeur d'Alene Mountain USGS quad also covers the area.
Trail contact: US Department of the Interior, Bureau of Land Management, Coeur d'Alene Field Office, 3815 Schreiber Way, Coeur d'Alene, ID 83815; (208) 769-5000

Finding the trailhead: From Coeur d'Alene drive east on I-90 for 10 miles to exit 22. Take the exit and head south and west on SH 97 for 2.4 miles (passing the Mineral Ridge Trailhead at 2.2 miles). Turn left off SH 97 onto FR 438 and go 0.4 mile to the junction with FR 1575 (Elk Mountain Road). Turn left on Elk Mountain Road and drive approximately 3.8 miles to the unmarked trailhead. The trailhead is at the point where Elk Mountain Road crosses Mineral Ridge. There is a wide parking area at the trailhead but no other facilities and at present no sign. The elevation at the trailhead is 3,180 feet. A GPS receiver may be a big help in finding this out-of-the-way trailhead. FR 1575 is often deeply rutted, and a high-clearance vehicle will probably be necessary to reach this trailhead safely. GPS: N47 36.805'/W116 39.427'

The Hike

From the wide parking area at the unmarked trailhead, the Lost Man Trail descends to the west, through Douglas fir, grand fir, and western larch woods. Within a few yards the track makes a switchback to the right, as you continue downhill at a moderately steep rate. After five more switchbacks the course reaches the Silver Wave Viewpoint at 3,020 feet elevation. There is a bench here as well as a good view to the north and east. The I-90 freeway is far below in the bottom of the valley.

Below the Silver Wave Viewpoint the tread continues its descent, making three more switchbacks as you cross the steep semi-open hillside to the junction with the Wilson Trail, next to the Bluebird Viewpoint. The Wilson Trail is to the left; the viewpoint is on a side path to the right, 20 feet from the trail junction. This junction is 0.4 mile from the trailhead on Elk Mountain Road, at approximately 2,900 feet elevation, so you have descended nearly 300 feet to get here.

A bench at the viewpoint makes this a great place to spend a few minutes and enjoy the view. Just past the bench is a rock outcrop that hikers often step up onto to get a slightly better view. If you step up onto this rock, be very careful: The rock can be slippery, especially when it is wet, and there is some exposure to the north and east. A fall could be serious.

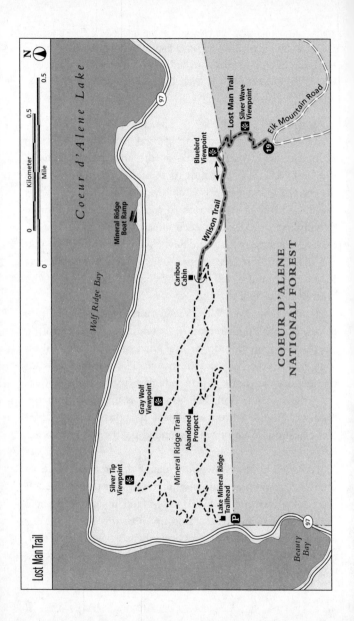

Lost Man Trail

N

Coeur d'Alene Lake

Wolf Ridge Bay

97

Mineral Ridge Boat Ramp

Silver Tip Viewpoint

Gray Wolf Viewpoint

Mineral Ridge Trail

Abandoned Prospect

Caribou Cabin

Wilson Trail

Bluebird Viewpoint

Lost Man Trail

Silver Wave Viewpoint

Lake Mineral Ridge Trailhead

P

COEUR D'ALENE NATIONAL FOREST

Beauty Bay

97

Elk Mountain Road

19

0   0.5   Kilometer
0   0.5   Mile

Once you are done admiring the view, step back to the junction and head west on the Wilson Trail. The Wilson Trail traverses a steep semi-open slope, but the trail itself is a far more moderate grade than the Lost Man Trail. After traversing the slope for 0.2 mile the route reaches the ridgeline of Mineral Ridge. As you reach the ridgeline you may notice an abandoned trail to the left that heads southeast up the ridge. This trail was once a roadbed and is still marked as a road on some maps. Bear slightly right, staying on the Wilson Trail, and in a little less than 0.2 mile you will reach the junction with the Mineral Ridge National Recreation Trail (Hike 18) at 2,780 feet elevation, 0.8 mile from the trailhead on Elk Mountain Road.

There is a water fountain at the junction, and a few yards west on the Mineral Ridge Trail is the Caribou Cabin. After inspecting the cabin and maybe sitting on the bench next to it and having lunch, retrace your steps back to the trailhead.

Miles and Directions

0.0 Hike west from the unmarked trailhead on Elk Mountain Road (FR 1575).

0.4 Turn left on the Wilson Trail next to the Bluebird Viewpoint.

0.8 Turn around at the junction with the Mineral Ridge Trail.

1.6 Return to the trailhead on Elk Mountain Road.

20 Caribou Ridge National Recreation Trail

This fairly strenuous climb up Caribou Ridge passes several viewpoints. As you climb, you travel through a widely diverse mixed conifer forest, maybe flushing out a grouse along the way. The lower 2.6 miles of this trail is generally rougher, rockier, narrower, and steeper than the upper 2 miles.

Distance: 9.2 miles out and back

Hiking time: About 5 hours

Difficulty: Challenging

Trail surface: Dirt, rough and rocky in spots

Best seasons: Summer and fall

Other trail users: Hikers only

Canine compatibility: Dogs are permitted but must be under control.

Fees and permits: None

Schedule: 24/7

Maps: The Coeur d'Alene Mountain USGS quad covers the area. The National Geographic Idaho topo on CD-ROM also covers the area but shows this trail somewhat inaccurately, as does the USDA Forest Service Idaho Panhandle/Coeur d'Alene National Forest map.

Trail contact: USDA Forest Service, Coeur d'Alene River Ranger District, Fernan Office, 2502 East Sherman Ave., Coeur d'Alene, ID 83814; (208) 664-2318

Special considerations: This is the most difficult hike described in this book. There is some exposure in places, so children must be kept well under control. Water is only available at the Beauty Creek Campground and the Mount Coeur d'Alene Picnic Area and Trailhead.

Finding the trailhead: Drive east from Coeur d'Alene on I-90 for about 10 miles to exit 22. Take this exit and head south and west on SH 97 for 2.4 miles. Turn left off SH 97 onto FR 438 and drive

0.6 mile southeast to the Beauty Creek Campground and Trailhead. The trailhead is on the right, just as you enter the campground. There is limited parking at the trailhead; restrooms and drinking water are available in the campground. The elevation at the trailhead is 2,160 feet. GPS: N47 36.447'/W116 40.173'

To arrange a car shuttle to the Mount Coeur d'Alene Picnic Area and Trailhead and make this a one-way hike, go back out to FR 438 and turn right (southeast). Follow FR 438 for 3.8 miles to the junction with FR 453. Turn right on FR 453 and drive 2.4 miles to the end of the pavement and the junction with FR 439. Turn right on FR 439 and go 2.3 miles to the trailhead. Be sure to bear right 0.1 mile after leaving FR 453 and stay on FR 439. The other road looks better here than does FR 439. FR 439 is a dirt road and is a little rough and rutted in places, but it can generally be navigated with a standard passenger car with a little caution. A high-clearance vehicle makes it much easier. There is somewhat limited parking, water, and a restroom at the trailhead. GPS: N47 35.141'/W116 41.459'

The Hike

The Caribou Ridge Trail (Trail 79) heads south across the grassy creek bottom as you leave the trailhead. Soon the track begins to climb. You quickly make a switchback to the left as the route ascends the slope covered with Douglas fir and western red cedar. A little less than 0.3 mile from the trailhead, the trail makes a switchback to the right. Half a mile into the hike, at 2,400 feet elevation, there is a view through the trees of the Beauty Creek Valley and the parking area at the trailhead. The course makes a switchback to the left 0.1 mile farther along. At the turn there is a view to the northwest of Beauty Bay (an arm of Coeur d'Alene Lake). Another 0.5 mile up the trail is another switchback. In this area the tread is quite narrow in places and somewhat exposed. Keep a close eye on the children here.

There will be a steep switchback to the left 1.8 miles from the trailhead. Here a poor path goes straight ahead to the southwest; don't take it. Make the switchback and hike another 0.2 mile to the Beauty Creek Overlook. No sign marks the overlook, but there is a good view of Beauty Creek Valley. At the viewpoint you will have climbed to 2,950 feet elevation.

The route reaches a junction with an abandoned four-wheel-drive road 0.6 mile past the viewpoint (2.6 miles from the trailhead). There are no signs at this junction, elevation 3,160 feet. Turn left on the road and continue to climb. Soon the roadbed disappears as you continue up Caribou Ridge. The trail makes several switchbacks as you ascend to another trail junction 0.9 mile farther up the ridge. This junction is also unsigned; bear right and stay on the main trail. It's a good idea to stop a few yards farther up the trail and turn around and look back at this junction. Make a mental note of what it looks like coming back down so that you don't take the wrong trail on the return trip, which would be fairly easy to do.

After you've hiked 4.2 miles, 0.8 mile above the last trail junction, the course bears right off the ridgeline that you have been generally following since passing the Beauty Creek Overlook 2.2 miles back. The tread now traverses the forested slope, heading west for the 0.4 mile to the junction with FR 439 at the Mount Coeur d'Alene Picnic Area and Trailhead. This is your turnaround point at 4,030 feet elevation, 4.6 miles from the Beauty Creek Trailhead. If you haven't arranged for a car shuttle, retrace your route back to the Beauty Creek Campground and Trailhead.

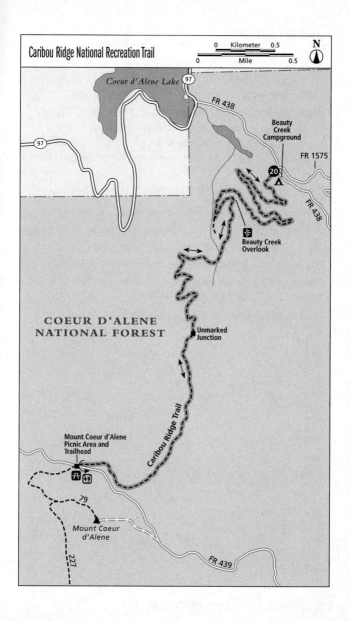

Caribou Ridge National Recreation Trail

0   Kilometer   0.5

0   Mile   0.5

N

Coeur d'Alene Lake

97

FR 438

Beauty
Creek
Campground

FR 1575

20

FR 438

Beauty Creek
Overlook

97

COEUR D'ALENE
NATIONAL FOREST

Unmarked
Junction

Mount Coeur d'Alene
Picnic Area and
Trailhead

Caribou Ridge Trail

79

Mount Coeur
d'Alene

227

FR 439

Miles and Directions

0.0 Hike southwest as you leave the Beauty Creek Campground and Trailhead.

2.6 Turn left at a junction with a four-wheel-drive road.

4.6 The trail reaches the Mount Coeur d'Alene Picnic Area and Trailhead and the junction with FR 439. If you have not arranged for a car shuttle or are not going to continue to the summit of Mount Coeur d'Alene, this is your turnaround point.

9.2 Return to the Beauty Creek Campground and Trailhead.

Options: Combine this route with the Mount Coeur d'Alene hike (Hike 21) to make a 10.9-mile out-and-back trip, or arrange for a car shuttle to the Mount Coeur d'Alene Picnic Area and Trailhead and make it only a 4.6-mile one-way trip. If you are going to continue to the summit of Mount Coeur d'Alene, turn right on FR 439 and walk a short distance west to the trailhead.

21 Mount Coeur d'Alene

Hike through the Douglas fir, grand fir, western hemlock, western white pine, and western larch forest to the cabin at the summit of Mount Coeur d'Alene.

Distance: 1.7 miles out and back

Hiking time: About 1.5 hours

Difficulty: Moderate but short

Trail surface: Dirt singletrack

Best seasons: Summer and early fall

Other trail users: The lower part of the trail up to the junction with Trail 227 is open to hikers only. Above there, horses are allowed, as are two-wheeled vehicles at certain times of the year.

Canine compatibility: Dogs are permitted but must be under control.

Fees and permits: None

Schedule: 24/7

Maps: The Coeur d'Alene Mountain USGS quad covers the area. The National Geographic Idaho topo on CD-ROM covers the area and shows this trail fairly well, as does the USDA Forest Service Idaho Panhandle / Coeur d'Alene National Forest map. The Forest Service map is, however, very small scale.

Trail contact: USDA Forest Service, Coeur d'Alene River Ranger District, Fernan Office, 2502 East Sherman Ave., Coeur d'Alene, ID 83814; (208) 664-2318

Finding the trailhead: Drive east from Coeur d'Alene on I-90 for about 10 miles to exit 22. Take this exit and head south and west on SH 97 for 2.4 miles. Turn left off SH 97 onto FR 438 and drive southeast for 4.4 miles to the junction with FR 453. Turn right on FR 453 and drive 2.4 miles to the end of the pavement and the junction with FR 439. Turn right on FR 439 and go 2.3 miles to the trailhead. Be sure to bear right 0.1 mile after leaving FR 453 and stay on FR 439. The other road looks better here than does FR 439. FR 439 is a dirt road and is a little rough and rutted in places, but it can generally be navigated with a standard passenger car with a little caution. A high-clearance vehicle makes it much easier. There is somewhat limited parking, water, and a restroom at the trailhead. The elevation at the trailhead is 4,030 feet. GPS: N47 35.142′/W116 41.487′

The Hike

As you leave the Mount Coeur d'Alene Picnic Area and Trailhead, the Mount Coeur d'Alene Trail (Trail 79) heads west-southwest through the picnic area. You soon pass a short spur trail, which leads to the outhouse, as you climb through the hemlock, fir, and larch forest. The track makes a sweeping turn to the left and heads southeast 0.2 mile from the trailhead. The route continues to climb gently as you pass a few scattered western white pines mixed in with the other conifers. The junction with Trail 227 is reached slightly more than 0.5 mile from the trailhead. At the junction you will have climbed to 4,260 feet elevation. A sign here states that it is 0.3 mile to the summit of Mount Coeur d'Alene.

Bear left at the junction and continue to climb gently. In just under 0.3 mile you will come to the junction with a four-wheel-drive road. Turn right on the road and walk a short distance to the summit and cabin. Just before reaching the cabin there is an open flat area on the right. This area could have once been used for parking when the road was open. The cabin is in rather poor condition, with shotgun holes through its metal skin. The elevation at the summit is 4,398 feet, and you are a little over 0.8 mile from the trailhead. This is the turnaround point, so when you are ready, retrace your steps back to the trailhead.

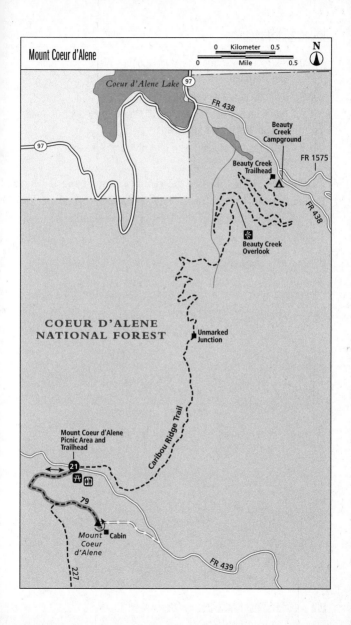

Mount Coeur d'Alene

0   Kilometer   0.5
0   Mile   0.5

N

Coeur d'Alene Lake 97

FR 438

Beauty
Creek
Campground

FR 1575

Beauty Creek
Trailhead

97

FR 438

Beauty Creek
Overlook

COEUR D'ALENE
NATIONAL FOREST

Unmarked
Junction

Mount Coeur d'Alene
Picnic Area and
Trailhead

21

Caribou Ridge Trail

79

Mount
Coeur
d'Alene

Cabin

227

FR 439

Miles and Directions

0.0 Hike southwest from the Mount Coeur d'Alene Picnic Area and Trailhead.

0.5 Bear left at the junction with Trail 227.

0.8 The route reaches the summit of Mount Coeur d'Alene. Turn around and retrace your steps.

1.7 Return to the Mount Coeur d'Alene Picnic Area and Trailhead.

Options: This hike can be combined with the Caribou Ridge National Recreation Trail (Hike 20) to make a long out-and-back hike from the Beauty Creek Trailhead.

22 Mullan Military Road Interpretive Trail

The Mullan Military Road Interpretive Trail is a short loop hike passing the spot where the historic Mullan Tree once stood. The US Army built a wagon road from Fort Benton, Montana, to Fort Walla Walla, Washington, between 1859 and 1862. Lieutenant John Mullan and his crew built 30 miles of this road in 1861, changing the route and going north of Coeur d'Alene Lake. Lieutenant Mullan carved the date FOURTH OF JULY 1861 on a tree, commemorating their construction reaching the pass and inadvertently naming Fourth of July Summit.

Distance: 0.5-mile lollipop loop
Hiking time: 30 minutes or less
Difficulty: Easy
Trail surface: Singletrack gravel
Best seasons: Summer and early fall
Other trail users: Hikers only
Canine compatibility: Dogs must be kept on a leash.
Fees and permits: None
Schedule: 24/7

Map: The map in this book is all that is needed for this short loop.
Trail contacts: USDA Forest Service, Coeur d'Alene River Ranger District, Fernan Office, 2502 East Sherman Ave., Coeur d'Alene, ID 83814; (208) 664-2318. Silver Valley Office, 173 Commerce Dr., Smelterville, ID 83868; (208) 783-2363.

Finding the trailhead: Take exit 28 off I-90, 16 miles east of Coeur d'Alene, at Fourth of July Summit. Turn east on FR 3097 on the north side of the freeway, following the signs. Go 0.3 mile, then turn right and drive another 0.2 mile on the entrance road to the parking

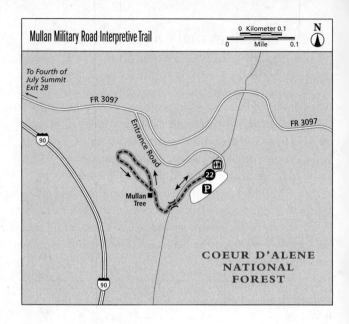

area and trailhead at 3,010 feet elevation. Plenty of parking and a restroom are available here. GPS: N47 37.196' / W116 31.013'

The Hike

The gravel trail descends slightly leaving the parking area. Douglas firs, grand firs, western white pines, western red cedars, western hemlocks, and Engelmann spruce tower above the tread. The course soon makes a turn to the right and crosses a bridge over a small creek. Across the stream the route quickly reaches a reader board that discusses Lieutenant John Mullan. A few yards past the reader board, turn right at a trail junction and begin the loop portion of this hike.

Soon the trail crosses a sometimes-wet area then reaches a bench. Bunchberries grow next to the trail here. A few feet farther along, the route bears left on the bed of the old military road. There is another reader board here, which gives you some details about the military road. A few yards farther along, the Mullan Tree Memorial will be on the right. After reading about the Mullan Tree, continue your hike a short distance to the trail junction that ends the loop. Hike straight ahead at the junction and return to the trailhead and parking area.

Miles and Directions

0.0 Hike south from the Mullan Tree Historic Site, Trailhead, and Parking Area.

0.1 Turn right at the trail junction to begin the loop.

0.4 Hike straight ahead at the trail junction, ending the loop.

0.5 Return to the Mullan Tree Historic Site, Trailhead, and Parking Area.